Behave'n Kids Parent Guide

Mini Methods or Madness

Small steps that
make BIG changes in
your kids' behavior

Janie and Roger Peterson

Behave'n Kids Press, Inc.
Omaha, Nebraska

D1167083

Published by Behave'n Kids Press Inc.
8922 Cuming Street
Omaha, NE 68114
402-926-4373
www.behavenkids.com

Library of Congress Control Number: 2006931750

Cataloging-in-Publication Data

Peterson, Jane L.
   Mini methods or madness : small steps that make big changes in your kids' behavior / Janie and Roger Peterson.
   p. cm.
   Includes index.
   "Behave'n kids parent guide."

   1. Discipline of children.   I. Peterson, Roger W.
II. Title.

HQ770.4.P4666 2006   649'.64

Project coordination and book design by Concierge Marketing Inc.
Written and Edited with Ginny Hermann
Illustrations by Jack Kusler and Jessica Wachtler
Printed in the United States of America

10 09 08 07 06   *   6 5 4 3 2 1

Dedication

This book is possible because of the wonderful parenting challenges that our three daughters posed. Molly, Macy and Katie, thank you for giving us so many opportunities to praise and be proud of your accomplishments and especially thank you for helping us refine our parenting techniques. We love you.

Other Books By
Janie Peterson

ISBN: 0-9714405-0-6 $16.95

ISBN: 0-9385107-3-8 $29.95

www.behavenkids.com
and at your favorite retailer.

Acknowledgements

Thank you to the many people who helped in the creation of this parent handbook. Ginny Hermann, for your patience and talents as a writer, Drs. Steve and Connie Taylor for sharing your time in editing for scientific content, Jim Norris, Kristen Massman, Amy Johnson, Tom Dowd and Julie Cornell for providing input on the first draft. Thank you to all the great staff and parents at Behave'n Day Center for your tenacity in using these techniques. Lisa Pelto's perseverance and friendship. And a special thank you to Jessica Wachtler for her cover illustration.

About Behave'n Day Center, Inc.

Behave'n Day Center, Inc. is committed to providing early intervention services to children with severe or chronic behavior problems. The goal of the Behave'n program is to assist and support the success of children at home, at school and in the community. Behave'n Day Center, Inc. is dedicated to work together with each child's family and community to enhance the child's success.

We developed training programs for parents and teachers in the following areas, and can customize a presentation for virtually any group.

- How to make sleeptime successful for you and the children.
- How to, how much, how effectively to discipline.
- How to teach play, sportsmanship and sharing.
- How to teach toilet training and make it successful.
- How to build (or rebuild) strong relationships with parents.
- Hitting, kicking and biting – How to work with the aggressive child.
- How to take a trip to the store without begging and temper tantrums.
- How to teach your child to be good during church services.

About the Authors

Janie and Roger Peterson, both licensed therapists, have spent their entire careers working with families, parents and caregivers to create a more nurturing environment for today's children.

The Peterson's speak across the nation to large and small groups of parents, caregivers, teachers, administrators and other professionals. They share their techniques, insights and wisdom to groups such as Council for Exceptional Children, Head Start, schools, Parent Teacher Groups, and many others.

www.behavenkids.com

What do professionals say about Mini Methods?

Over the years, I have read so many books on child rearing but none captures the essence of Time-In/Time-Out like Mini Methods does.

This nicely detailed approach to parenting is so refreshing. I think the Petersons have done the best job of discussing the importance of time-in and how best to do time-in of virtually any book that I have read. It sounds as if they have spent hours in my office listening to me trying to encourage parents to be more positive with their children.

Mini Methods or Madness is bigger than a booklet but a little smaller than a lot of books, yet chock full of good suggestions for parents.

Thank you so much for writing this important book. I'm sure that it will be well received by the parents who are privileged to read it.

Ed Christophersen, PhD
Children's Mercy Hospital
Kansas City, Missouri

And...

What becomes perfectly clear in the days, weeks and months after having a child is that the labor involved is never over. Parenthood, from its defining moment of inception, is a labor of love. So too is this book – Mini Methods or Madness. Based on the underlying belief that a positive and consistent approach to discipline provides the most important foundation for successful teaching – a belief I firmly share – The Petersons have taken their years of experience and their approach to helping children to outline an easy to understand, realistic to apply, step-by-step approach to managing your child's behavior. Their Mini Methods are sure to make big changes – not only in your child's behavior, but in your understanding and parental expectations as well. With techniques that emphasize "yes," and minimize the energy you and your child waste on the inevitable "no," this parenting guide is sure to help you as you lead your own children down the path to lifelong success.

Dr. Laura Jana, M.D., Omaha, Nebraska
Author of "Heading Home with Your Newborn"
Published by the American Academy of Pediatrics

Contents

Resources:

1

Introduction to
Mini Methods

Little Anna is a delightful 3-year-old. Her curly brown hair, big brown eyes and adorable giggle make her irresistible to nearly everyone who crosses her path. She's incredibly smart, loves to play and is very compassionate for a child her age, but she has a major problem. Whenever Anna's parents take her into a public place, she can't resist touching things. It starts the minute she hits the door. At the grocery store, she fills her arms full of candy. At the mall, it's toys. In the hobby store, it's plastic flowers. At a restaurant, it's mints. At Grandma's, it's antique dolls. The worst part is that Anna refuses to follow directions and put the items back.

"No, Anna. Put the candy back," Dad says. "No!" Anna replies, as she places the candy next to the cash register.

"No. We are not buying any new toys today. Please put the cars back," Mom pleads.

"No!" shouts Anna, stomping her little foot.

"No, no, no, Anna. Do not touch Nana's dolls," says Grandma. "They are very old, sweetheart."

"No, Nana! My dolls," Anna exclaims, as she rushes into the bathroom clutching the dolls and closes the door behind her.

It's gotten to the point where Anna's parents avoid taking her anywhere because they know every visit will end with a struggle. Although they know it's wrong, Mom and Dad sometimes give in and let Anna have what she wants just to avoid a scene. Spending a few extra dollars is better than the humiliation of having everyone hear Anna screaming "No! No! No!"

Nearly all parents have experienced a power struggle similar to this one with their own children. Whether it's grocery store battles, bedtime arguments, homework issues, mealtime struggles or any of a hundred other parent/child conflicts, most moms and dads find themselves going to battle with their children over what should be simple lessons of right versus wrong.

These loving parents try their best to train their children to be good, responsible adults. They model, teach, listen, react and give their children love and attention, yet the struggles continue. What are these parents doing wrong? Is there a secret ingredient to successful parenting? The answer to this question is yes, and the secret is simpler than you may think. The fact that you are reading this book means you want to do the best you can for your child. Think back and ask yourself one question. What was your child's first word? Take a moment to remember.

If you're like most parents, shortly after mastering "Da-da," "Ma-ma" and the obligatory "Coo-kie," your little angel probably learned to say "No." The word "No" is a favorite tool in nearly every parent's disciplinary toolbox. We consider it our job to watch for inappropriate behavior and remedy the situation with a stern look, a shake of the head or a clear, sharp "No."

Because young children tend to model language and attitudes after their parents, before you realize it, your precious baby is flexing his verbal and emotional muscles by shaking his head, furrowing his brow and twitching his little finger while reciting, "No, no, no." So, what's the problem? We've found that a parent who chooses to correct a child's misdeeds by dwelling on the naughty actions teaches by emphasizing disobedience. This approach

> Get over the idea that only children should spend their time in study. Be a student so long as you still have something to learn, and this will mean all your life.
>
> – Henry Doherty, American Business Leader

gives more "weight" to inappropriate behavior and lessens the importance of the child's positive, agreeable moments. But never fear. There is a better way.

If you're looking for a positive, more loving approach to teaching, you've come to the right place. Our goal is to help you learn how to work with your child to create a family environment based on respect and harmony – an atmosphere that embraces "Yes."

If practiced consistently and correctly, the strategies and methods you will learn in this book may not only strengthen and enhance your family relationship but might also change your life and the life of your young child forever.

When our oldest daughter, Molly, was born, our goal was to avoid negative teaching tactics and the behaviors associated with them. We made a conscious decision that the first word out of her mouth would be "Yes." The birth of our second daughter, Macy, and the adoption of our foster daughter, Katie, prompted us to fully commit to a teaching style that focused on our children's good behavior and downplayed disobedience. As mental health professionals, as well as parents, we were thrilled to find that our approach worked.

As professionals in the field of children and mental health, we later established a day center that focuses on caring for children with severe behavior issues. In our efforts to emphasize the positive aspects of behavior in our center, we devised a caring teaching method based on our first-hand experience with our own daughters and with the hundreds of clients we have worked with through our careers. The method enhances good conduct by showering children with extensive amounts of parental praise and attention in response to "good" behavior; naughty behavior is downplayed by offering no rewards and limited verbal and physical responses. This "secret" to successful parenting puts the emphasis on "Yes" rather than focusing on "No, No, No."

This program is loosely based on the popular Time-In/Time-Out principle of teaching, a proven disciplinary approach that is the subject of many parenting books and magazine articles. Although existing research proves Time-In/Time-Out works, our method incorporates a number of effective, new components that can help make this approach work faster and more convenient for you to carry out.

This teaching method, which began in the early 1980s as a way to teach proper conduct to our own daughters, has evolved into a highly effective approach to training that has helped many concerned parents guide their children toward good behavior, while establishing strong, loving family connections. Because these steps have been so successful for us in both our personal and professional lives, we wrote this book to share the process with others who want to incorporate this powerful teaching method into their own families.

In the case of books, the point is not to see how many of them you can get through, but rather how many can get through to you.

— Mortimer Jerome Adler, educator

This book is your guide to enhancing your relationship with your child. You will also learn the behavior adjustment process and why it works. You will also learn:

- How practice paves the way to success,

- The importance of establishing a rich Time-In relationship with your child,

- A 3-step disciplinary process that helps teach acceptable behavior, and

- Guidelines to get you started.

Each chapter concludes with a Fast Facts section that summarizes the most important information in each chapter. These review sections are perfect for quick reference after you've finished the book. You'll also find exercises sprinkled throughout the book to help you understand and apply these new principles. Each exercise was carefully designed to help you get the most out of the material, so please take the time to complete them as you work through the book. There are also quotes that will tickle the funny bone, touch the heart and stimulate the mind.

This program is best suited for parents with young children from 18 months to 9 years old and successful with children who exhibit very mild to extremely severe behavior problems. Although younger children are ideal for this approach, the basic principles of the program can work well with some older children and those with mild to moderate developmental delays.

It is best to follow the steps outlined in the book as closely as possible to ensure success. Because each child learns and responds differently, we've given you options that enable you to determine the approach that works best for your child. As you read through each chapter, we will make it clear which steps must be followed to the letter and which allow a more personal touch.

It is essential that you read this entire book at least once, cover to cover, completing the exercises as you go, before beginning the process. We want you to use this book to your advantage, so don't be afraid to highlight sentences, write in the margins or do anything else to help you make it your own (unless, of course, it's a library book or you've borrowed a copy from a friend). This will enable you to get the most out of the book and will help you modify each section to fit your unique family situation.

Although the steps outlined in this book have proven successful with most youngsters, some children may need help from a licensed therapist or clinical psychologist familiar with Time-In/Time-Out processes. If at any time you think you need help handling your child's behavior, don't hesitate to call a mental health professional.

2

The Program and Why It Works

What does your child value more than anything else in the world? If you're taking a mental tour through your house, weighing one possession over the other, take a moment to stop and look in the mirror. The one thing your young child desires most is you. Your undivided attention is worth much more than the new bike your child got for his birthday or the baby doll she sleeps with every night. Talking, reading, hugging, praising or simply watching your youngster is the most powerful reward you can give to your child. Private time with you fills your child with more warmth and love than any inanimate object ever could.

Everybody today seems to be in such a terrible rush; anxious for greater developments and greater wishes and so on; so that children have very little time for their parents; parents have very little time for each other; and the home begins the disruption of the peace of the world.

– Mother Teresa

Because most children revel in adult interaction, their little minds quickly learn how to get as much attention from their parents as possible. The key to enhancing positive actions and redirecting misbehavior is granting this attention appropriately. Let's take a look at two parents and their differing approaches to dealing with their children's misbehavior.

Parent One, Scott, leads a busy life. He and his wife juggle demanding careers, a growing family, a full social and church calendar and a household that needs constant attention. After work, he finds just enough time to help get dinner on the table, bathe his daughter and read her a book before bedtime. Weekends are filled with grocery shopping, laundry and a long list of errands. This loving, dedicated father devotes as much time as possible to his child, but because of his hectic schedule, he practices a no-nonsense approach to teaching and discipline. Whenever his little girl is naughty, he talks, yells, explains and negotiates with his daughter in an effort to teach her right from wrong. When she exhibits good or neutral behavior, he might occasionally make a positive comment, but after all, that's how he expects her act. Why praise her for doing what she is expected to do?

Parent Two, Anne, a single mother of 3 boys, also feels the pressure of her family's hectic schedule. Between her stressful job, unending housework, constant meal preparation and a calendar packed with baseball practices and piano lessons, she barely finds time to sleep. But when interacting with her kids, Anne consciously focuses on her sons' positive actions, rather than on their negative conduct. When Anne sees her sons acting in a good or acceptable manner, she rewards them with compliments, kisses, hugs and other forms of affection and attention. When the children commit minor infractions, she essentially "turns herself off" by withholding attention for a very short time until the children comply.

Now, which parent is focusing on enhancing positive behavior while strengthening the relationship with her children? Anne, of course. As our example illustrates, Anne offers ample amounts of praise when her sons are behaving well and very little attention when they are naughty. This usually results in an overall increase in good, positive behavior. On the other hand, through his actions, Scott says, "I'll give you my attention when you act out and will withhold it when you're nice," which usually results in more disorderly behavior. After all, to a child, negative attention is better than little or no attention at all.

If you see more of yourself in Parent One than Parent Two, you're not alone. Unruly behavior is much more noticeable and is easier to identify than appropriate behavior, so we tend to focus on our children's negative actions and downplay the moments when they are cooperative.

So how did we get this way? Well, look at it like this: How many times has a traffic cop pulled you over to congratulate you for driving within the speed limit or for making a good, safe turn? It's probably never happened because that's not how our society works. We are expected to follow the rules with little or no encouragement or pats on the back from authority figures. Instead, we usually get feedback only when we've done something wrong, like running a red light or arriving late to work.

Look for the good in every person and every situation. You'll almost always find it.

– Brian Tracy, business coach

As parents, we tend to teach in the same manner we ourselves have been taught. Thus, Parent One is much like a traffic cop, "pulling his daughter over" only to discuss her misdeeds rather than to praise her good actions.

It's hard to admit, but punishment can be much easier to give than positive support. When we spank and yell, it feels like we are "doing something" about our children's misbehavior. While lashing out is shorter and can cause an immediate effect, this teaching approach does not work in the long run, and it can have a very detrimental effect on a parent/child relationship. It also teaches children that spanking, hitting, yelling and other aggressive behaviors are acceptable ways to resolve differences. Our goal with this book is to teach you how to help your child in a manner that is both effective and long lasting. Don't worry -- it's never too late to transform your parenting style by adopting a positive, loving manner. Make the commitment that today is the day you change your teaching approach forever.

The most effective time to teach proper behavior is when your child is being good because this is when he is most open to you and your suggestions. By consistently noticing and celebrating favorable behavior, you put the emphasis on the positive aspects of your child. Giving attention during the "good times" rather than the "bad times" not only rewards your child but also changes the way you feel and act toward him. Focusing on the positive also teaches your child to interact with others in an upbeat, respectful manner. This style of communication ultimately encompasses all aspects of the child's life, from interacting with other children on the playground to establishing lasting connections with siblings, teachers and others. And, keep in mind that the actions you take to improve your parenting style today set the stage for your child's own parenting style well into the future. A positive attitude toward teaching is very powerful indeed. It's never too late to redirect your teaching method from a negative approach to a positive one. Beginning today, make the commitment to look for the good in your child.

Fast Facts

The one thing a child wants more than anything else is attention from his parents. The proper use of this attention is the key to enhancing positive actions and redirecting misbehavior.

Offering ample amounts of praise when children are behaving well and very little attention when they are naughty usually results in an overall increase in good, positive behavior.

Inappropriate behavior is much more noticeable and easier to identify than appropriate behavior, so parents need to look for the "good" times and praise them.

It's never too late to redirect your teaching method from a negative approach to a positive one.

Exercises
Where are you now?

I am happy. I am finally starting to relax and enjoy being a parent and really getting to know the brighter side of my son. Everyone comments on his new behavior and outlook on life – teachers, doctors, friends and family.

The first step of any journey is realizing where you are starting from. Before you begin a new approach to teaching your child appropriate behavior, you first need to identify which behaviors you want to change. Most parents have a long list of actions they would like their children to improve upon, but, when asked, they often come up with sketchy descriptions of behaviors that are too general or too difficult to pinpoint. For example, "I want him to obey me" or "I want him to respect me more" are valid complaints, but they are too far-reaching and unfocused. Please remember that your growing child is a work in progress. He needs small, easy-to-attain goals, especially when working under a new teaching system like this one, so he (and you) will be more likely to succeed.

Get a piece of paper and make a list of the behaviors you want to help your child correct. Make these actions very specific and appropriate to your child's age. Some examples may include not following directions, refusing to eat at meal time, fidgeting, interrupting phone calls, using unacceptable words or lying. After you have made your list, number the behaviors, with

#1 being the behavior that bothers you the most,

#2 second-most,

#3 third-most and so on.

The behavior you list as #1 will be our first teaching goal. We will tackle your child's most irritating behavior first because once you tackle this one, the rest of the list will be easy. After you master the steps outlined in this book, you will also be better equipped to tackle the less troublesome behaviors quickly and efficiently. Be sure to keep this list on hand; you will need to refer to it throughout this book.

3

Practice Makes Perfect

Let's pretend you've just bought a new piano and want to learn to play your mother's favorite song in time for her birthday party, which is just 10 months away. You've had the instrument properly tuned, found a qualified instructor and have already taken your first lesson. Bring on the birthday cake! You're ready to perform, right? Wrong!

As we all know, mastering the piano, playing softball, working algebra problems or learning any other new skill requires dedication, commitment and hours and hours of practice. Learning to teach your child using praise and rewards is no different. For many of us, verbally and physically praising our children on a regular basis is new, uncharted territory, much like learning a foreign language or exploring a new neighborhood. Concentrated practice is the key to your success.

Many a good man has failed because he had his wishbone where his backbone should have been.

– Unknown

The more often we practice a behavior or skill, the better we get at performing that action.

The Importance of Practice

The more often we practice a behavior or skill, the better we get at performing that action. For example, if you spend 2 hours a day on the tennis court perfecting your serve, lob and backhand, you'll probably beat the pants off a first-time player because you consistently practice the moves necessary to play a winning game of tennis. On the other hand, if you lounge on the couch 15 hours a day watching television and playing video games, you'll excel at avoiding physical activity because you actively practice a sedentary lifestyle. These examples illustrate how repeated performance results in a more successful outcome, making you more proficient at the actions you perform most frequently.

Well, it's the same when you communicate with your child. A parent who is more accustomed to correcting her children than complimenting them gets better and better at being critical and less and less adept at being complimentary. On the other hand, the parent who consciously chooses to praise and reward her children gets better at praising and is ultimately more successful at communicating with them.

This example works equally well when children are in the driver's seat. When kids practice being naughty, they get really good at it. The naughtier they are, the more practice they get, which ultimately results in a child who is proficient at being unruly, disobedient and unmanageable. This is where you, the praising parent, come in. It is your job to help your children practice being good by becoming skillful at using positive attention to praise and reward them.

When and How to Practice

The most effective time to practice favorable behavior with your child is when he is being good. When your son is playing nicely, eating quietly at the dinner table or sharing a favorite toy with his brother, he is much more open to you and your suggestions than he is in the heat of a naughty moment.

Children are the sum of what parents contribute to their lives.

– Unknown

He is much more willing to listen and learn when he is calm than when he has just bitten his sister or spit milk across the room. Why? Well, here's an example: Think about the last time you had a heated argument with your spouse or significant other. Did you really listen to what the other person was saying? Were you concerned about how your language was making the other person feel? Do you even remember what the argument was about? When emotions are high and your mind is running on overdrive, you don't communicate well and rarely hear what is being said. This is exactly how it is with our children. To them, we are much like the adults in Charles Schulz's popular Peanuts comic strip. The "wah, wah, wah" of a trombone is all Charlie Brown, Lucy and the gang hear whenever a parent, teacher, neighbor or other adult speaks. This is exactly how we come across to our children when we yell and scream at them.

Talking with your child when he is behaving appropriately, such as sitting patiently in the car or making his bed, is ideal. These calm, peaceful moments offer the perfect opportunity for you to set your household rules and help your child practice good, acceptable behavior. Offering your attention and guidance during the "good times" rather than during the "bad" rewards your child while providing gentle teaching moments that stick with him and make a lasting impression.

Neutral behaviors are actions your child already does well. These are skills the youngster has already mastered and performs as a matter of habit. So let's say you see your daughter quietly coloring a picture at the dining room table and realize this is a prime time to practice some good behavior. Now what? Take 5 minutes, sit down with her and practice behavior you want to teach. An exchange to encourage sharing may sound something like this:

The Scenario: Mommy sees 4-year-old Molly coloring a picture at the dining room table. Mommy walks up and says:

Mommy: "Hi, Molly. You sure are doing a good job coloring that picture. I really like how you used the red and brown on the puppy's nose. Hey, let's play a little game. Let's pretend I am your little sister and I want to share your crayons. I'll color this picture of some flowers while you color that puppy, and we'll practice sharing, okay?"

Molly: "Okay, Mommy. That sounds like fun."

(Mommy sits down with Molly at the table.)

Mommy: "Great. Now, I am going to use the blue crayon on my picture and you use the red one on yours. I'll color this tulip with my blue crayon, and I'll color this daisy blue, too.

(Mommy and Molly color together for a minute, then Mommy says:) I think this rose would look pretty if I colored it red, but you are using the red crayon, right?"

Molly: "Right!"

Mommy: "How about I hand you my blue crayon and you hand me your red one. We'll share the crayons, okay?"

Molly: "Okay, Mommy. Here you go."

(Molly and Mommy trade crayons.)

Mommy: "That's great. I really like it when you say 'okay' when I ask you to share. It makes me feel good and I bet it makes you feel good, doesn't it?"

Molly: "Yes, Mommy."

(Mommy gives Molly a big hug.)

Mommy: Now, you color with the blue one and I'll color with the red one. Isn't it fun to share, Molly?"

Molly: "Yes, Mommy. What colors should we share next?"

Mommy: "Why don't you choose the colors this time."

Molly: "Okay, Mommy."

Well, that's it. A successful practice session focusing on sharing. Mommy uses simple words, a caring attitude and a little gentle guidance to teach Molly the proper way to share. Take a moment to notice how Mommy makes it clear they are practicing the act of sharing by repeating the word "share" numerous times throughout the practice session. She also works through the process of sharing step-by-step, giving Molly the tools she needs to handle sharing in the future. Mommy also praises Molly for responding with an "Okay, Mommy." The "Okay" response is a great habit to teach children because it not only let's you know your child heard you, but it also shows good manners and respect. This little scenario is age-appropriate, easy to complete

A mother's love for her child is like nothing else in the world. It knows no law, no pity, it dares all things and crushes down remorselessly all that stands in its path.

– Agatha Christie
mystery writer

25

and takes about 2 minutes to act out, but the lasting effects of the exercise remain long after the crayons are put away.

Short practice sessions like this one help children understand what is expected of them and offer the perfect opportunity to role-play tricky situations before they come up in everyday life. And if the two of you butt heads over sharing in the future, you can refer back to the practice session, remind your child how easy it was to share and how good the process made you both feel.

Make Practice a Priority

Taking a few minutes out of your day to practice good behavior is an excellent way to teach acceptable social skills. Just 5 minutes a day will do wonders, but you are probably wondering how you're supposed to find time to practice good actions with your kids. Most parents are already so busy, they just can't add one more thing to their day. If you feel this way, then ask yourself this: How much time do you spend nagging at your children? How many minutes do you waste each day ignoring your kids when they pester you or misbehave? Five minutes? Ten minutes? More?

These lost moments get you nowhere. Many parents end up feeling like a hamster on a wheel, expending tremendous amounts of energy only to end up exactly where they started, with naughty, disrespectful children.

Why not try something different and schedule time in your day to practice behaviors with and to teach your children? You undoubtedly practice effective time management skills in other areas of your life. None of us would get through a day at the

The best inheritance a person can give to his children is a few minutes of his time each day.
– O. A. Battista, author

office or an afternoon running errands without setting priorities and establishing a game plan. Why not try similar tactics in your family life? Prioritizing and making time to actively teach your children what you want them to learn establishes a pattern of positive communication that will pay off long after the lessons are complete. And be sure to continue practicing good behaviors even after your child has mastered them. If you work several short teaching sessions into your daily routine, you'll quickly begin to notice how fruitful your efforts become.

As we mentioned earlier, this entire process should be an enjoyable, positive experience for you and your children. The practice sessions enable you to give your kids the attention they crave while offering you the chance to teach basic social skills as you get closer to them emotionally. Your children will love it, and you will too.

Fast Facts

- Practice is the key to success when learning any new skill.

- The more often you practice a skill, the better you get at performing it.

- A child who practices good actions on a regular basis becomes more skilled at acceptable behaviors.

- The most effective time to practice proper behavior with your child is when he is being good because this is when he is most open to you and your suggestions.

- Practicing proper behavior with your children involves using simple words, a caring attitude and a little gentle guidance to teach the actions you want him to learn.

- Make time to practice acceptable behavior with your children by making it a priority. Schedule practice time like you would any other necessary daily activity.

- Your practice sessions should be fun for you and your child. These teaching moments will offer the perfect opportunity to connect with him emotionally as well as physically.

Exercises
Where do you want to go?

I am amazed at how well these methods work and wish all families could learn them as well as enforce them. It would make their lives easier. It is a relief to me to know I do not have to get worn out by screaming at my son or regretful for all the spankings he would've gotten.

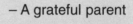

– A grateful parent

The next step in our journey is deciding where you want this trip to end. After all, if you don't have a destination, how do you know when you have arrived? Each parent has his or her own definition of which behaviors are okay and which are not. For example, one parent may tolerate her child running rampant through a pediatrician's waiting room, moving chairs, jumping over ottomans, ripping magazines and rough-housing with other children.

"What's the big deal?" the parent says. "At least he isn't hitting his sister."

Another parent in the same waiting room may have higher expectations of his child, allowing her to leave her seat only for a quick sip of water or a trip to the bathroom.

Neither parent's rules are "right" or "wrong." They simply have different expectations of their children while waiting to see the doctor.

Now it is time to decide what you are going to expect from your child before you embark on your teaching journey. Examine the list of your child's behaviors you want to change and write a short description of the action you want your child to perform in each situation. Ask yourself this: "In this circumstance, exactly what do I want my child to do?" Now write the answer next to each behavior on the list. For example, if your list includes "Interrupts me while I'm on the telephone," write an exact description of an action that is an appropriate substitute for interrupting a phone call.

Your replacement behavior list for interrupting phone calls might look like this:

1. Taps me gently on the arm one time.

2. Waits quietly.

3. I ask him what he wants.

4. He replies.

Making these decisions and breaking your expectations into steps before you begin provides a framework for teaching and helps you recognize when your child is making progress.

Work your way through your list, writing desirable behaviors alongside the undesirable ones. Keep in mind as you proceed that you can always make adjustments if you find your expectations are too high or too low. To help you get started, we have included a list of sample behaviors and steps to mastering these skills in the Resources section at the back of this book.

Once you have identified your ideal replacement behaviors, you are ready to practice these actions with your child. You should focus on one goal at a time, so commit to focusing on the behavior you listed as #1 on your list. Choose a time when your child is relaxed and seems open to having some focused fun, then create a game of "Let's Pretend" for the two of you that teaches the behavior you outlined in the exercise. Be explicit by going step by step with your child through your desired action, making it very clear exactly how you want your child to react in this "pretend" situation.

Make time to practice this new behavior with your child at least 5 times (yes, 5 times) a day until you are sure he understands what is expected of him. The time that you share during these practice exercises is very important for both of you, so don't rush or short-change yourself. Cherish these moments and enjoy yourself, knowing that you are nurturing a positive parent/child relationship.

4

Praise and Rewards

When many parents begin to notice problem behaviors in their children, they turn to television talk shows, parenting magazines and the Internet for the newest disciplinary approaches and guidelines. Others seek advice from friends, relatives and the family pediatrician to help regain control over their rambunctious youngsters, but what most parents don't know is that the secret to turning

Children need your presence more than your presents.

– Jessie Jackson

most naughty kids into well-behaved children lies within. Most behavior problems can be remedied by establishing a positive approach to family communication using a little flattery, a tender smile, an occasional treat and a whole lot of love.

The power behind this teaching method is the proper use of Time-In, a highly effective, caring approach to teaching young children right from wrong. Time-In is the opposite of its more popular alter-ego, the Time-Out, a widely utilized disciplinary method that moves a child into a quiet area for calming in the event of naughty, negative behavior. On the flip-side, the term "Time-In" describes the process of giving a child positive attention, verbal praise and small prizes (like a cookie or penny) as a reward immediately following favorable behaviors. Smiling, laughing, playing, hugging, dancing, snuggling, reading, singing – these are all examples of Time-In at its best.

In this book, the words "praise" and "rewards" are used to describe the rich, effective Time-In experience. Praise and rewards are important teaching tools for parents because, when practiced consistently and correctly, they serve as the primary method of increasing good behavior and preventing inappropriate behavior.

Now, you're probably shaking your head in disbelief. How can smiling and hugging be more powerful deterrents than threatening and yelling? Shouldn't parents present themselves as authority figures in order to gain respect and instill the fear necessary to control young children? Absolutely not. Research shows consistently praising and rewarding children is much more effective in the long term than negative approaches to parenting.

Think about the last time your spouse, boss, parent, friend or significant other complimented you on a job well done. Take a moment to remember the situation. How did that attention and recognition make you feel? Appreciated? Loved? Proud? Important? Worthwhile? Although the entire exchange probably consisted of only a few friendly words, a big smile or a pat or two on the back – a minute or two at the most – the moment was undoubtedly meaningful to you and continues to supply you with warmth and pride. This is the effect you are striving for when sharing rich praise and rewards with your child. A kind word, a touch on the head, a "good job" spoken at an opportune time –that's what praise and rewards are all about.

Setting Rules for a Happy Household

Let's pause for a moment to address the difference between a positive parenting approach and leniency. When we talk about lavishing positive attention on your child, we are not implying that strict rules are not necessary. Parents who are "pushovers" are asking for trouble. A recent study examining how parental style affects child

My mother's menu consisted of two choices: take it or leave it.

– Buddy Hackett,

behavior found parents with a "strict, yet warm" parenting style produced the most well-behaved children. Why? Because establishing a rigid set of rules and enforcing them with a caring approach results in a household where expectations are clear and the consequences for disobeying the rules are understood. Setting the ground rules in advance and utilizing a teaching method that enables you to work with your child rather than to gain control over your child opens the door to a happier, more stable home life.

What are "Neutral" and "Developing" Behaviors?

Throughout this book, we encourage praising neutral as well as developing behaviors, but how do these actions differ? Let's begin by defining both terms, then we'll look at why praising both actions is helpful to you.

Neutral behaviors are actions your child already does well. These are skills the youngster has already mastered and performs as a matter of habit. For example, if your daughter regularly says "please" and "thank you" without prompting, you should consider it a neutral behavior. If your son usually eats dinner without incident, this is also considered a neutral behavior.

So why is it necessary to recognize and praise the neutral, everyday moments your child has already mastered? Although neutral behaviors may not seem significant, praising them offers you the chance to acknowledge and maintain

All kids need is a little help, a little hope and somebody who believes in them.
— Ervin "Magic" Johnson, Basketball legend

these good actions while setting the stage for new, positive behaviors. Providing your daughter with occasional praise for seemingly insignificant tasks also ensures that you won't lose track of skills she has already accomplished.

We don't expect our children to be perfect all of the time, so if we consciously look for and acknowledge neutral behaviors, we give ourselves more chances to give kids the praise and love they deserve. Offering a "good job" to little Sarah for getting into the car, going directly to her booster seat and fastening her safety belt without first squeezing into the driver's seat, stopping to honk the horn and readjusting the mirror also sends the message that even the simplest compliance can result in extra love and attention.

In addition, some parents of especially difficult children may find it nearly impossible to find behaviors to praise. By first focusing on neutral behaviors, these parents discover something positive to acknowledge while establishing praise and rewards into their family structure. If little Lindsay is a challenging child, but she regularly brushes her teeth and goes potty before bedtime without incident, she has mastered these neutral behaviors and deserves a pat on the back.

Developing behaviors are any new skills you are teaching your child. These desired actions include any activity or response that is positive, helpful or simply acceptable. If a child who regularly throws a temper tantrum at the grocery store makes it through one aisle tantrum-free, she has just performed a developing behavior. If a usually defiant youngster picks up 3 toys when asked to clean up his room, he has also just performed a developing behavior.

Praising developing behaviors is beneficial to the teaching process because it gives parents the opportunity to physically and verbally reward children for performing new tasks we hope will become second nature. Making a big deal of even the tiniest new, positive action helps your child learn what you expect from him and how he can trigger exciting, favorable reactions from you. For example, if you've spent the last 3 months asking little Ryan to stop knocking on the fish tank, then you suddenly notice him gazing thoughtfully into the aquarium without touching the glass, then walking quietly away, the tyke has accomplished something! He deserves a big "atta boy" for trying this new behavior and giving the poor guppy a break.

Make the Connection

Offering kind words for both neutral and developing behaviors gives you more opportunities to connect with your child and emphasize acceptable actions.

It's as simple as that! In addition, the kind words and actions associated with praise and rewards work to cement the connection between parent and child. And here's

I've been very blessed. My parents always told me I could be anything I wanted. When you grow up in a household like that, you learn to believe in yourself.

– Rick Schroeder, child star

some really good news: When taught consistently, developing behaviors will evolve into recurring neutral actions and become part of your child's personality. She will perform good behaviors because she wants to, not because she is praised for them. So make a conscious effort to actively focus on both neutral and developing skills and acknowledge them. You'll notice a favorable difference in your child and in yourself.

Praise and Rewards 101

Now, it's time to move on to the nitty gritty of praising and rewarding. Let's say you notice your young child performing a neutral or developing behavior. What should you do next? First, you need to be aware that this is the time to act. Timing is essential, so immediately following the developing or neutral action, offer some sort of verbal or physical praise.

> **W**hen I was a kid, I got no respect. When my parents got divorced there was a custody fight over me, and no one showed up.
> – Rodney Dangerfield, comedian

It is imperative that you give praise right after your child's positive or neutral behavior. Why? Humans learn by consequence, so we see our circumstances as directly related to our actions. This is how we learn. For example:

When we turn the faucet, the water starts running. This is cause and effect. "If I do this, then that other thing will happen." You can provide your child with all of the praise and rewards you want, but if you let even one minute pass before you give them, he probably won't tie the praise to his good action. On the other hand, if the child is rewarded immediately after completing developing and neutral behaviors, it won't take long for him to figure out that his actions are responsible for your favorable reactions. So don't wait. The minute you see a praise worthy behavior, jump on it! Give your child all the love and attention you've got.

Your child just performed a praise worthy behavior and it's time for you to take action. What you say and do next is crucial, and it all depends on what type of action your child has achieved. This is when many parents make mistakes that end up working against their best intentions, so it's important to understand what to say and do for both developing and neutral behaviors.

If your child has just performed a new, developing behavior, go "bonkers." Give him tons of verbal and physical praise in addition to a small material reward to show him how proud you are of his accomplishment. Now is the time to make a positive impact on your child and reward him for his good action, so the bigger and more animated you are in your praise, the better. Be sure to lavish your child with praise and love each and every time he performs the new behavior. This is where some parents get into trouble. If you are inconsistent in how often you give praise for developing behaviors, your child probably won't understand the benefit of learning these new actions. On the other hand, if you praise him every single time he performs a developing behavior, he'll begin to want more and more of these fun, exciting moments, which will ultimately result in more new, developing behaviors.

If your child has just performed a neutral behavior, a verbal acknowledgment or a tiny hug or kiss is sufficient. Praising neutral behaviors should occur every now and then to serve as a reminder that her ongoing "goodness" does not go unnoticed. Although it is important to recognize neutral behaviors occasionally, these little congratulatory moments should be spread out and should not include material rewards. If you make a big deal out of behaviors your child already has "under her belt," she is likely to regress and expect a floor show from you every time she performs the smallest good deed. By noticing neutral moments and randomly praising them, you help your child stay on the right track while setting the stage for new, developing behaviors.

The important thing to remember is that, although you offer praise much more frequently for developing behaviors, the quality of your attention should remain the same for the successful completion of both neutral and developing behaviors. You should strive to be energetic, warm and sincere every single time you offer praise and rewards to your child.

> The longer we live the more we think and the higher the value we put on friendship and tenderness toward parents and friends.
>
> – Samuel Johnson, 18th Century English author

The Ins and Outs of Verbal and Physical Praise

Verbal praises are very effective and can be given virtually anywhere. Here are some examples of what verbal praise sounds like:

- "Wow, Michael. You are really good at pouring. Look at that perfect glass of milk. You didn't spill a drop. Excellent!"

- "I really like how you are sharing that game with your sister, Mitchell. It is so much more fun to play together, isn't it?"

- "Great job going potty all by yourself, Amanda. What a big girl you are. I am so proud of you."

Physical rewards can include a big hug, a "high five," kisses on the head or any other loving gesture you choose. Keep in mind that your goal is to make the child feel happy and proud of herself, so strive for actions that mean something to her. It is also acceptable to give your child a material reward as a token of your appreciation. A penny, sticker, animal cracker or other small symbol will let her know you noticed the good deed and that you care.

If you choose to give your child a little "treat" now and then as a reward for good behavior, don't feel guilty about it. This isn't bribery. Parents who bribe children give a prize before the action to encourage good behavior. You are choosing to give a token following good behavior to reward your child for already acting in an acceptable manner. This powerful approach to teaching does not "pay" children to act nicely. Instead, it offers you a method of teaching that enhances the precious relationship between you and your child.

Another great way to acknowledge your child is to let her help you complete a task. Most children love to help their parents. It makes them feel trusted and valued, so the next time your daughter does something good, ask her to help you stir the pancake batter or dry the dishes with you. Her face (and her heart) will beam with pride!

It is important to remember that praising and rewarding your child should be fun for both of you. Create your own personal praising and rewarding style. Make it your own by using words and phrases that are meaningful to you and your family. Make up songs, tell a joke, fall down laughing, jump up and down. Be silly. Your kids will love it. And be sure to vary the rewards and praise you give. Children love

A child reminds us that playtime is an essential part of our daily routine.

– Unknown

surprises, so mix it up. Making the learning process exciting only reinforces your good efforts. If you run out of ideas, we've included a list of free and inexpensive rewards in the Resource section in the back of this book for inspiration.

Phasing Out and Moving On

Remember to make a big deal out of new, developing behaviors, but once a behavior shows signs of changing into a neutral behavior, ease up on the praise and focus on your next teaching goal.

Here's an example of how this works: Remember when your child first learned to use the potty? The first few weeks your son successfully used the bathroom, you probably turned cartwheels in your excitement, but once he understood the concept and began going all by himself, you probably gave him the "thumbs up" every now and then, but you eased off on the circus maneuvers and moved on to other goals.

This is how it should be with praise and rewards. Offer big praise in the beginning when the acceptable behavior is developing, then ease off until the action becomes yet another neutral behavior.

Becoming a Praising Parent

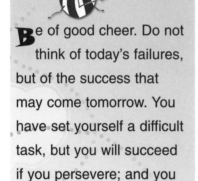

Be of good cheer. Do not think of today's failures, but of the success that may come tomorrow. You have set yourself a difficult task, but you will succeed if you persevere; and you will find a joy in overcoming obstacles.

– Helen Keller

Now, if all of this sounds uncomfortable to you, keep in mind that the more you praise your kids, the easier it will become. And never forget that children have an uncanny ability to detect insincerity. If you don't believe in what you are saying and doing, neither will they, so avoid being dishonest or condescending in your praise at all costs. The minute your children realize you are being phony is the moment your credibility goes flying out the window.

Teaching acceptable behavior by using your love and attention is the most important step you will learn from this book. We can't stress strongly enough how significant and effective this step can be. Although the techniques described here may sound simple to master, it takes effort to get into the habit of praising and rewarding correctly and consistently. We all want to establish good, strong relationships with our children. Communicating with our kids effectively not only helps us open up to them, but it also presents us as more likable in their young, impressionable eyes. Giving our time and attention also lets our children know we not only love them, but we like them as well.

Your ultimate goal in this journey is relationship-building and mutual respect. Offering kind words and actions to your child is the first step in a process that is as empowering for you as it is for your child. The love and praise you give will draw you and your child closer and create a significant bond that lasts a lifetime.

Fast Facts

Praise and rewards describe ways a parent can use his positive attention or a small material reward to improve a child's behavior.

Research shows a strict, yet warm parenting style produces the most well-behaved children because children know the household rules and what is expected of them.

Neutral behaviors are skills your child has already mastered and performs as a matter of habit.

Developing behaviors are first-time activities or responses that are positive, helpful or simply acceptable.

It is essential to praise and reward both neutral and developing behaviors.

It is imperative that you praise your child immediately following a neutral or developing behavior so she will tie the praise and attention to her positive action.

How you offer praise depends on what type of behavior your child has just performed.

For developing behaviors, give a great deal of verbal and physical praise in addition to a small material reward. Be sure to lavish your child with praise each and every time she performs a developing behavior.

For neutral behaviors, a verbal acknowledgment or a tiny hug or kiss is sufficient. These small displays of attention should occur occasionally to help your child avoid falling into her old habits.

Strive to be energetic, warm and sincere whenever you praise a neutral or developing behavior.

Verbal praise includes short phrases that let your child know you noticed his good behavior and you are proud of his accomplishment, no matter how small it may be. Physical praise can include a big hug, a "high five," a kiss on the head or any other loving gesture you choose.

The process of praising and rewarding your child should be fun for both of you. Create your own style and be sure to vary the rewards you give to keep it exciting for the child.

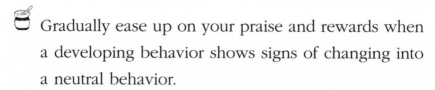 Gradually ease up on your praise and rewards when a developing behavior shows signs of changing into a neutral behavior.

Avoid being dishonest or condescending in your praise.

The more you praise and reward your children, the easier it gets – for you.

Exercises
How do you want to get there?

He is now under control. listens, pays attention and is a much happier child. And let's not forget that I'm now a much happier mother!

– A grateful parent

Okay, so you know where you are and you know where you want to go. Now it is time to decide how you want to get there. We will arrive at our destination using praise and rewards for making positive steps toward the desired behaviors you listed earlier. Take a look at your list again, but let's just focus on #1, your first behavioral goal. It is time to turn this developing behavior into a neutral behavior.

Make a commitment to watch your child and be prepared for when he performs the target behavior successfully. This step is where you hold up your end of the bargain by praising him wholeheartedly when it occurs. Let's return once again to our "Interrupts me when I am on the phone" example. After practicing how you want him to behave when you are on the phone and you've rewarded him for waiting, you will get to the point where a light bulb clicks on in your head when he reacts correctly. This is your cue to praise.

Now is the time to set up a successful scenario for your child. Right after the two of you have completed a practice session, call a friend for a quick chat. Make it obvious to your child that you are on the phone by remaining in his field of vision and maintaining close contact with him during the call. Most likely, your child will see you performing the actions you just practiced, and he will follow the rules you just outlined in your practice session by tapping you once on the arm and standing quietly until you ask what he wants. You will then ask what he wants and he will tell you. When all of these steps are met, go nuts! Hug him, kiss him, jump around, dance, sing, give him a cookie and let him know, without a doubt, that he did something spectacular.

Immediately after you have calmed down, go directly to your notebook and start a Praise Log. This log will consist of the date and time when you praised your child, what you praised him for and how you praised him. Your Praise Log might look something like the example that follows:

Date/Time: January 13 — 3:45 p.m.

I praised Jimmy for tapping me on the arm one time, then waiting for me to ask him what he wanted when I was on the phone.

I praised him with a big kiss, a happy dance, a hug and a chocolate chip cookie.

If tables work better for you than journaling, you can modify your entries to look like this:

Date/Time	Behavior	Reward
01/13 3:45pm	Tapped me on the arm and waited before interrupting me on the phone	Kiss, dance, cookie

This Praise Log will help make you aware of how often you praise your child and how he is making progress. If your expectations are clear and your praise is consistent and genuine, you will likely notice your child using these developing behaviors in other situations, such as when you are talking to someone face-to-face or when you are busy at the computer. When the right behavior happens, remember to heap on the praise. If you offer praise or rewards consistently and correctly, you will see positive results in your child. So keep yourself on track and don't miss an opportunity to offer praise for appropriate behavior.

5

Modeling

Six-year-old twins, Natalie and Maddison, spend time everyday playing "house." Natalie dusts the bookshelves, reads the newspaper and vacuums the carpet in the living room (her "house") while Maddison washes dishes, feeds her baby doll and cooks dinner in her "house" (the kitchen). They visit each others' homes for "coffee," chat on pretend telephones and borrow items from one house to use in the other. When their mother happens upon the action, she watches with amazement from the hallway as Natalie sits in Mom's reading chair to check the television listings and Maddison plays "spoon airplane" to feed her baby just like Mom did this morning with her baby brother. "Where did they learn all of this?" Mom wonders. "Are they really watching me that closely?" Well, Mom, the answer is yes!

The latest research reveals that modeling is one of the most effective teaching methods available. Modeling occurs when a person purposefully displays certain behaviors in hopes that others will imitate them. No direct "instruction" is necessary; instead, the "teacher" chooses to use actions and words he wants his "student" to incorporate into her own behavior. Through repeated "lessons," the child learns how she is supposed to act in a variety of situations. Modeling can also occur when someone goes about her daily routine without consciously choosing those behaviors she wants others to imitate, as the example illustrates.

Our children are watching us live, and what we ARE shouts louder than anything we can say.

– Wilfred A. Peterson, author

Behaviors can be strengthened, weakened or maintained by good modeling techniques. Modeling can be used to develop social skills (like being polite and assisting others), to teach appropriate behaviors (like following directions and waiting one's turn) and to enhance work skills (like being on time and finishing tasks), thus making the possibilities of teaching using modeling virtually endless.

Children often look to certain role models, like popular sports figures, movie stars, television personalities and singers, to set the standards for the way they act, talk, dress and wear their hair. Kids look to these "cool" people to help them develop personality traits that are accepted and envied by their peers. Although these influential individuals can inspire a child to act in both positive and negative ways, it is a child's parents who are the most powerful role models in her life.

One factor that makes modeling successful is the perceived importance of the person doing the modeling and the similarity between the "teacher" and the "student." The way a mother or father acts on a daily basis creates a type of blueprint for a child's life. When your child watches you react in everyday situations, she accepts your modeled behavior as the ultimate example of how to act. These elements make modeling an extremely successful tool for parents who want to instruct their children in acceptable everyday behaviors in a loving, hands-on manner.

Children learn many aspects of life from their parents. Not only do they learn how to react in day-to-day situations, but they also acquire many of their likes and dislikes from mom and dad, or adults that share in raising the child, such as a grandmother or foster parent. If you have a favorite football team, your child most likely roots for the same players. If you enjoy taking a bike ride every Saturday morning, it's a good bet that your daughter wants to ride alongside of you. If you have a passion for old movies, your son probably yearns to cuddle with you to catch an old flick. Even your choice of career has a great impact on your child. Just think of how many actors have children who follow in their footsteps or how many physicians have children who also become doctors. Why does this happen? Because the goals and accomplishments of parents become aspirations for their children as well.

As people grow older and become parents themselves, many notice the subtle influences of their own parents creeping into their interactions with their children. You have probably continued traditions with your children that you learned from your parents, such as sharing favorite meals, family stories, holiday activities and bedtime rituals you experienced as a child. But this type of modeling can work both ways.

How many times have you heard yourself criticizing your kids and thought, "Oh no. I sound just like my mother." Well, if your mother criticized and belittled you, she modeled these parental behaviors to you. By imitating them, you not only follow her model, but you also model these actions for your own child in the process.

It is imperative that you are always conscious of what you say and do in front of your kids. You have undoubtedly seen them imitating your mannerisms, facial expressions and language choices. Your kids want to be like you. They watch every move you make. When you act in a kind, gentle, responsible manner, your child perceives this as the best way to conduct herself, but when you act in a less-than-acceptable way, she thinks this behavior is acceptable for her as well.

Let's look at another example. Most parents who smoke know the dangers associated with the habit, so naturally they do not want their children to follow in their footsteps. However, the more the child sees her parent smoke, the more she thinks smoking is an acceptable thing to do. This is why the adage, "Do as I say, not as I do," does not work with children. Knowing this, examine how often you lose your temper in traffic, cut to the front of the line, blatantly lie or use inappropriate language in your child's presence. With each of these actions you teach your children that this is the way you want them to act.

Role modeling is the most basic responsibility of parents. Parents are handing life's scripts to their children, scripts that in all likelihood will be acted out for the rest of the children's lives.

– Stephen R. Covey, leadership guru

The best way to model good actions for your kids is for you to live the life you want them to live. If you want your daughter to go to college, set a good example by getting your degree. If you want your son to be physically fit, make the time to exercise yourself. If you want your children to eat their vegetables, eat your own. Know that you can try to tell your children what to do, but it's your actions that speak more loudly and clearly than any words you could use. It is that simple. When you take charge of your own actions, you'll take charge of your children as well.

Every child is made up of genetic pieces that help define who he is, but the environment you create in your home is instrumental to who your child will become. The sooner you consciously begin to model good behavior, the more effective your efforts will be. Young children look up to and want to be like their parents, but by the time they become teenagers, kids try to break from parental influences somewhat and look to their peers for guidance. Make the most of the influential years by modeling good behavior when your children are young – when your efforts will be most successful.

Try your best to make conscious decisions about how you act around your children. Because parents rarely sit down to teach social behaviors, relationship skills, survival skills and coping skills, you must show your child first-hand how life works. Model good behavior as situations come up, and you'll see great strides in your youngster. You'll undoubtedly find that your kids will do some things that aren't modeled by you, but they will most likely stick with the things they learn from you – good and bad. So, become the best you can be and set good examples. Live the life you wish for your child, and you will teach her how to live well.

FAST FACTS

🥁 Modeling occurs when a person purposefully displays certain behaviors in hopes that others will imitate those behaviors.

🥁 Modeling also occurs when someone goes about her daily routine without purposely choosing behaviors she wants others to imitate.

🥁 Modeling can be used to develop social skills (like being polite and assisting others), teach appropriate behaviors (like following directions and waiting one's turn) and enhance work skills (like being on time and finishing tasks).

🥁 Modeling is an extremely effective way for parents to teach good behavior to their children because youngsters look to their parents to provide an example of how they should act in the world.

🥁 It is imperative that you are always conscious of what you say and do in front of your kids.

🥁 The best way to model good actions is to live the life you want your children to live.

Modeling

 Every child is made up of genetic pieces that help define who he is, but the environment you create in your home is instrumental to defining who your child will become.

Exercises:
You're in the driver's seat

> **M**yself and my husband know how to appropriately deal with our daughter's negative behaviors without spanking and without feeding into her desire for negative attention. Her siblings are much happier, tension in the house has fallen dramatically, and everyone sees us working in a positive manner to improve behaviors.
>
> — A grateful parent

As we travel toward our final destination, it is important to always remember that you are in the driver's seat. You have the power to dictate where you are going, how fast you travel and when you arrive. All of the power is yours. This may sound great, but along with this power comes responsibility. Your greatest responsibility is to always be aware of what you are doing and how you present yourself to your child.

Modeling

In the next exercise, you will realize the extent of your power to influence your child and her behavior through modeling. Take some time to examine your actions during your next family meal together. How do you hold your fork? Do you rest your arm on the table? Do you use your napkin often? What do you usually drink? Then choose one of these habits and change it during your next few family meals. If you rest your arm on the table while eating, try keeping it in your lap. If you usually drink soda pop, switch to water. Try clearing your throat a few times. Then watch your child. Over the next few meals you'll begin to notice your child copying your new habit, probably without even asking you about the switch. This shows the control you have over her without uttering a single word.

Now, let's put modeling to work in an effort to reverse that irritating behavior you identified in our earlier exercises. You will teach your child your chosen desired behavior by modeling the exact actions you want your child to use in everyday situations. Using our example of, "Interrupts me while I'm on the phone," you want to replace the interrupting with tapping you once on the arm, then waiting quietly until you ask what she wants. You can model this behavior by interrupting someone else's call in your child's presence by following these rules yourself.

Let's say your spouse or friend is on the telephone and your child is nearby. Simply walk up, tap him on the arm one time and wait quietly until he asks what you want. Then ask your question, thank him for his answer and quietly walk away in full view of your child. Be sure to tell your spouse that you plan to interrupt his calls for the next few days so he won't be taken off guard by your actions. It is also important that your spouse responds in a manner that is consistent with how you plan to communicate with your child. This will reinforce the lesson even more. Perform this exercise for several days and you will see improvements in your child's actions in regard to this target behavior.

6
3 Steps to Managing
Naughty Behavior

We have concentrated thus far on ways to manage good behavior because we want you to look for and focus on positive actions whenever possible, but what happens when your young child acts up? First of all, don't take it personally. Every child has his naughty moments. Whether it's offensive language, physical aggression, outright disobedience or worse, you can count on your little angel getting into trouble no matter how much you hug and kiss her. Why? Because children learn by testing their boundaries and trying different approaches until they figure out which actions work for them. Find comfort in knowing that the manner in which you respond to these unfavorable actions determines whether your child repeats the undesirable behaviors or not. The power is entirely in your hands. How you react to naughty behavior is the key.

Lights, Camera, Reaction

All kids will use undesirable behaviors as a means to get their way. Let's look at a few scenarios and some typical parental reactions to these situations.

The Chatterbox

This morning little Julie woke up very early, sneaked into the kitchen and emptied the egg carton by throwing

Child rearing myth #1:
Labor ends when the baby is born.

– Unknown

the eggs, one by one, against the refrigerator. This action, although quite unusual, was exciting and fun for this rambunctious 5-year-old. Upon rising, Mommy finds the makings of a 12-egg omelet dripping down the fridge and is not pleased. She responds by spending 10 minutes lecturing Julie about why egging major appliances is unfit behavior. She then engages the child by helping her clean up the mess and finishes by hugging the sobbing girl to make her stop crying. If Mommy chooses to respond in this manner, she can expect Julie to continue smashing innocent dairy products all over the kitchen in the future. Why? Because Julie not only had fun throwing the eggs, but she also got exactly what she loves the most – her mother's attention.

The Clown

Ian's family affectionately calls him the "Little Tornado" because the disorderly 6-year-old leaves destruction wherever he goes. On most days, his room is a mess, the yard is scattered with balls, and the entire house is a collision course of toys. One day, Dad asks Ian to pick up his room, and the child responds with a loud, "No." Dad tries bargaining with the boy by offering to help him with the task; Ian once again responds with a sharp, "No." Dad then resorts to comical antics by morphing into a "Toy-Eating Dinosaur" while stomping around the room gathering up the toys.

After repeated requests, Dad finally cleans the room himself and, in the process, winds up looking weak and goofy to his impressionable young son. This dad made two mistakes:

1) he allowed Ian to ignore a simple request, thereby guaranteeing the boy will disobey in the future, and

2) he followed through by completing the task himself, telling the child that if he refuses Dad's request to clean his room, Dad will do it himself.

The Negotiator

Little Katie is a smart 2-year-old. She knows she shouldn't play with Mama's make-up, but the lure of the open drawer is too tempting to resist. She reaches in, grabs a tube and begins slathering her lovely lips in Cheery Cherry lipstick. When Mama walks in and sees her little beauty queen, she panics. Mama sweetly asks for her lipstick, but Katie continues to beautify herself. Mama then grabs a candy bar from the kitchen and offers to trade the chocolate for the lipstick.

If there were no schools to take the children away from home part of the time, the insane asylum would be filled with mothers.
– Edgar Watson Howe, American novelist

Katie, now finished with her makeover, gladly hands the make-up over and begins eating the chocolate, adding a lovely brown mustache to her already red face. Mama has just performed the old Bait and Switch, a method of bribery that replaces one object for another. Sure, Mama got her lipstick back, but in using this approach, she also rewarded Katie for playing with the lipstick, or at least that's how Katie sees it.

The Repeat Offender

Carlos is a smart 7-year-old who loves to read. He often steals away with a book for hours to escape to foreign lands or learn the intricate details of every reptile known to man. Unfortunately, Carlos doesn't always put his books away when he finishes with them. His parents know the importance of reading and encourage his passion for books, but they've grown tired of constantly picking up after their prolific reader.

One afternoon, Papa sees Carlos toss a book casually to the floor, so he asks the boy to pick it up. Carlos responds with a sigh. Papa once again asks Carlos to pick up the book; this time Carlos looks at  his father, but continues to ignore the request. After asking Carlos 10 times to pick up the book and receiving an equal number of brush-offs, Papa rises angrily from his chair and moves toward the boy. Finally realizing his father means business, Carlos jumps up, grabs the book and quickly places it in the bookcase.

Some may think this exchange is perfectly acceptable, but when Papa allowed Carlos to ignore his first request,

Never raise your hands to your kids. It leaves your groin unprotected.

— Red Buttons, comedian

he taught the boy that he doesn't have to listen and obey until his father gets angry. Papa could talk until he's "blue in the face," but the boy won't listen 95% of the time because he knows he doesn't have to. Sure, Carlos eventually follows Papa's direction, but not before forcing his father to the breaking point.

Do you see yourself in any of these scenarios? If so, join the club. It is normal for parents to do whatever it takes to stop naughty behavior as quickly as possible, but doing anything to avoid a bad reaction from your child is not the way to go. Avoiding tantrums and similar behaviors in the short term is not an effective way to teach your child right from wrong. In our examples, The Chatterbox talks to avoid a meltdown; The Clown uses his monster tactic to avoid a confrontation; The Negotiator trades candy for lipstick to avoid further destruction; and The Repeat Offender restates his direction over and over to avoid giving a consequence.

These solutions are successful when the parents' goal is to avoid an immediate meltdown, but they do not work to decrease undesirable behaviors in the long run.

Our examples also illustrate how children can shape their parents' behavior. The ideal parent/child relationship puts the parent, not the child, in the driver's seat. You must gain control over your situation by taking charge and determining how you plan to deal with the everyday ups and downs of parenting. Choosing how and when you react to your child is essential.

Teaching your child to follow directions quickly and efficiently sets him up for success inside and outside the family unit. Listening to instructions and completing tasks effectively pay off in the short term by helping your

A good plan today is better than a perfect plan tomorrow.

– George S. Patton, U.S. General

child become a better student, athlete, guest and friend; in the long run, these skills encourage your child to become a valued employee, neighbor, spouse and parent.

You are the primary teacher in your child's life; it is your duty to teach him right from wrong. If you tackle these issues now, you'll both enjoy the benefits for years to come.

It is always best to deal with naughty behaviors immediately so the child has the opportunity to learn from his mistakes. Each of our situations offers the perfect chance for the child to learn a new skill – Julie can learn to ask permission, Ian and Carlos can learn how to listen and obey, and Katie can learn to follow directions – but first their parents must learn the importance of allowing their children to feel and work through their anger.

Sure, your son will get mad when you insist he stop playing and clean up his room, but how else is he going to master such basic life skills as prioritizing and following directions? It's actually good for kids to get mad because this is how they learn to control their anger. As a parent, it is much easier to help a 3-year-old learn how to manage his angry feelings than to try to help a 13-year-old master this skill. The older your child gets, the more difficult his issues become, and the larger he is, the tougher it will be to handle his angry outbursts. So let your child get mad, then use these outbursts to your advantage. We'll teach you how to deal with your child's anger later in this chapter, but right now, let's look at some strategies you can use to limit your words and actions.

The Sounds of Silence

Teaching with few words and actions may sound crazy, but this approach is not only possible, it is also very effective. As mentioned before, children thrive on attention, but some kids cannot tell the difference between their parents' harsh negative attention and loving, positive attention. That's why we examined this issue in such depth in our discussion about praise and rewards. Pouring on the attention when your child is good and limiting your words when he is naughty is meant to set up a strong contrast between what he experiences when he is being good and how things change when he is disobedient.

If you choose simply to ignore your child when he is naughty and offer no extra attention when he is "good," his unfavorable behaviors will certainly decrease, but be aware that this change will happen very slowly. You'll also find his behavior will get

Children have more need of models than of critics.

– Joseph Joubert,
French moralist

much worse before it gets better because he is trying to get attention from you. However, when you choose to provide rich Time-In moments, loving praise, consistent rewards and lots of practice during the "good times" and withhold your words during the "bad times," you'll see unruly behavior decrease with longer lasting results.

Choosing when to talk and when to stay silent is one of the most important decisions a parent can make. Stopping inappropriate behaviors using a minimum of verbal and physical interactions is your "ace in the hole." This is what we will teach you now. You'll soon find when you use these strategies consistently and correctly, you will see results.

Okay, so you are probably thinking this all sounds great, but how much talk is too much? A good rule of thumb to follow is the One-Word-Per-Year-of-Life guideline. For example, since little Julie is 5 years old, Mommy's verbal response following naughty behavior should consist of just 5 words. Something like, "No throwing eggs at things," would work well. If Julie was 4 years old, Mommy could use 4 words like, "No throwing eggs ever." If she was 3 years old, 3 words like, "No throwing eggs," would be appropriate, and so on. This rule is easy to remember, simple to enforce and allows you to teach your child while offering a minimum of attention and language.

As you recall from the previous chapter, the best time to teach is when children are being good, but how is your youngster supposed to understand right from wrong if you react with very few words and actions during her naughty times?

Let's revisit our egg-tossing tot, Julie. When Mommy blew up over the "egg incident," she talked too much. The most important thing Julie learned from the 10-minute discussion and cleaning session was that throwing eggs gets Mommy's attention and it's fun. If Mommy had shortened her words following the incident, she would have given Julie a very powerful penalty. It's as simple as that.

> **I**f you talk to your children, you can help them to keep their lives together. If you talk to them skillfully, you can help them to build future dreams.
>
> – Jim Rohn, motivational speaker

Remember, you are what your child wants most. If you give tons of attention when your child is good and very little when she is naughty, you will build the extreme contrast needed to show her which actions are acceptable and which are not.

The Truth about Consequences

If you look back at the scenarios we just discussed, you will find they all have one thing in common: none of these parents required the child to experience a negative consequence for his or her naughty action. Setting a consequence for the child and sticking with it is the best way to get your point across while maintaining control over the situation.

Consequences often mean different things to different people, so let's agree that in the context of this book a consequence is an action a parent takes after a child's inappropriate behavior in attempt to decrease that behavior.

Sometimes I wish I were a kid again; skinned knees are a lot easier to fix than a broken heart.

– Unknown

As you remember, messy Ian has a habit of leaving toys around the house. Not only does he refuse to pick up his room, but he also sits idly by while his father does the work for him. If Ian's father had instead given a negative consequence to the boy for his lack of assistance, Ian would most likely remember the incident and be more apt to follow directions in the future.

When giving a consequence, many parents decide to take away something their child values, but giving consequences to young children can be tricky. It's easy to decide which freedoms and privileges are most valued by pre-teens and teenagers. Limited access to the car, an earlier curfew, loss of television time or restricted telephone privileges can make a big impression on older children, but what possession can parents take away from youngsters to make them feel the sting of consequence? The answer is ... nothing. There is no possession a parent can take away from a young child that can't be easily replaced.

Very young children live entirely in the present; the only thing that matters to them is what is happening right now. Most younger kids could care less if you lock away a favorite truck or baby doll; they will simply play with something else. Have you ever seen a child turn an empty cardboard box into a playhouse? If so, you've seen firsthand that young children don't need toys to make their own fun, so what is the answer? What is the one thing your child can't live without? Take another long look into the mirror because the answer, once again, is YOU. Your undivided attention is priceless because your child cannot replace it. That's why limiting your words and actions during the naughty times is so effective.

Many parents think scolding and yelling are negative consequences, but, as you've probably already noticed, the effects of verbal confrontations do not last, and they rarely result in a decrease in naughty behavior. Screaming matches also tend to work against a parent's authority. For example, think back to the last time you yelled at your child. Try to picture the situation. Who was most upset by your verbal outburst – you or your child? If you are like most parents, you were probably much more rattled by your scolding than your child. Why? Because (1) the child wasn't listening, and (2) the child didn't lose anything. If anything, he gained attention from you, which is exactly what he craves. Losing control not only gets your blood pumping and makes you appear vulnerable, but it also leaves you feeling guilty for losing your cool and embarrassed for being mean. So do yourself a favor and stop the shouting. A calm, controlled response is much more effective.

Dealing with Everyday Challenges

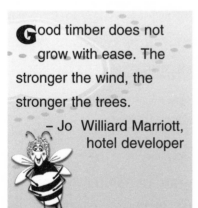

Good timber does not grow with ease. The stronger the wind, the stronger the trees.

– Jo Williard Marriott, hotel developer

One difficult situation every parent must deal with is the temper tantrum. Any parent who has tried to quiet a screaming child in the grocery store or at the mall can relate to the feelings of helplessness and loss of control that can fluster and embarrass even the most hard-nosed mom or dad. Children are notorious for throwing tantrums at the most inopportune times, and it is up to you to decide how and when to act. The best thing you can do is to remove your child from the situation as quickly and quietly as possible. Shutting off your words and leaving the area with your child the instant a tantrum rears its ugly head will show him that this behavior will not be tolerated.

A good number of parents are quick to report that their children do not have temper tantrums. We hate to burst these proud parents' bubbles, but most children have temper tantrums. This is how children express themselves. If your child has never thrown herself on the ground, kicked, screamed, spit, cursed and shown other behaviors associated with the classic temper tantrum, she is simply using alternate strategies to show her displeasure. Some of the less obvious tactics children use to show their tempers include laughing during a confrontation or blatantly ignoring a parent's requests. Although these behaviors are not "classic" temper tantrums, they are evidence of defiance and prove the child is not listening.

As you can see, temper tantrums can disguise themselves as other, less blatant behaviors, so don't be fooled. And remember, these "hidden" tantrums, as well as the classic kicking and screaming kind, help your child get his needs met every time. And what does he need? Your undivided attention, of course! To end this cycle, you must stop the behavior in its tracks by dealing with these problems right after they occur. If that means leaving a full cart of groceries in the middle of the store to give a consequence when your child throws a tantrum, then so be it. The short-term pain of abandoning a full grocery cart to leave with a screaming child is nothing compared to the long-term gain of returning with your well-mannered child in the future.

It is also important to avoid that age-old parental mistake of warning your child. Most parents fall into the trap of repeatedly warning their kids of impending consequences because they see these threats as a way to teach while avoiding giving a punishment. Unfortunately, these warnings don't work. The words you use when threatening your child go "in one ear and out the other." These warnings also give her more of what she really wants – your attention. Let's look at some classic warnings and see why each one is a losing battle:

"If you don't stop pulling the cat's tail right now, you're going to be in big trouble."

Showing your child that he won't get a consequence for his unacceptable action as long as he stops it immediately means he can do whatever he wants and he won't get in trouble. If your child is doing something naughty, he should

If evolution really works how come mothers only have two hands?

– Ed Dussault

already be in trouble. Telling him to stop rarely decreases unacceptable behavior, and it doesn't ensure that, even if he does stop, he won't be inclined to do the same thing in the future. Children need to learn that "Stop" means stop. Now!

This lesson not only can save your sanity, but, in some situations, it could also save your child's life. When you catch your child doing something naughty, you need to give a consequence immediately with no warnings, no negotiations and no deals. It's the consequence that stops the behavior, not the words. So stop talking and start acting.

"How many times have I told you not to run in the house?"

This phrase is probably one of the most misused sentences in the parental language book. Your parents probably used it on you. If they did, think back and remember if it worked. If you're like most kids, it probably didn't. When you give warnings like this one, be prepared to receive a smart-mouthed answer from your precocious child in return. The "How many times…"

You can learn many things from children. How much patience you have, for instance.

– Franklin P. Adams, American Journalist

phrase puts the power in your child's hands. It not only encourages her to contribute to the conversation, but it also reminds her that she has chosen to ignore your requests in the past. The best way to respond to repeated refusals to obey your house rules is to give consequences immediately and unceasingly until the child learns to obey the first time.

"You'd better stop that by the time I count to 3 or else. One…two…!"

The purpose of the warning count is to delay or avoid an inevitable consequence. Parents who count teach their children that they don't have to obey until the parent gets to "3." This strategy defeats the purpose of teaching the child the importance of listening and obeying immediately when the parent speaks. Research shows that counting can be effective, but it only works if the parent always follows "3" with a consequence. As we see it, the numbers "1" and "2" are actually warnings, which we just discussed, so why delay the inevitable? The best reaction to naughty behavior is immediate action with no warnings and no counting.

It's time to move on to our 3-step disciplinary method, but before we introduce anything new, let's review the rules we have set thus far:

- Limit your words when your child is naughty.

- Use the One-Word-Per-Year-of-Life guideline to help you stay on track.

- Don't be afraid to give a consequence for naughty behavior.

- Refrain from yelling at your child.

- Do not warn.

Three steps to Success

No matter how good you get at praising, rewarding, giving consequences and limiting your words, your child is still going to get into trouble. It's inevitable. That's why we devised this 3-step method to lovingly teach your child how to behave. As mentioned earlier, giving a consequence to little kids can be difficult, but the steps outlined here offer an easy-to-learn, simple-to-use teaching method that discourages naughty behavior, controls anger and strengthens the relationship between you and your child. And, because of its subtle, non-physical nature, you can enforce this method virtually anywhere, and most people will be unaware you are doing it.

Good parents give their children roots and wings. Roots to know where home is, wings to fly away and exercise what's been taught them. – Jonas Salk, microbiologist who discovered polio vaccine

You should try to follow the steps illustrated here as closely as possible unless we tell you there is room for adjustment.

We'll begin with a detailed explanation of the 3-step teaching process. Then we'll examine how to teach the process to your child.

Let's Get Started!

You are about to learn a series of steps (or consequences) that serve as a way to prevent naughty behavior; each step in the chain is designed to be more serious than the one before. The first step is called the Mini, the second step is called the Chair and the third step is called the Time-Out. These steps, along with the careful use of your attention, work together to create a blueprint for handling naughty behavior ranging from the tiniest slip-up to the most severe infraction. They also offer you an effective way to teach your child proper behavior in a loving, protective manner, making you less likely to spank or yell.

The keys to your success are:

(1)   giving a consequence for naughty behavior

(2)   limiting your attention when the child is completing one or more of the steps and

(3)   following the rules outlined here.

Now, let's get started with the first step — the Mini.

THE MINI

The very first step in the disciplinary sequence is called the Mini. This short yet effective disciplinary measure requires an immediate response by both parent and child in the event of naughty behavior. A Mini is used when a child first shows a naughty behavior, like not listening, refusing to obey, ignoring a request or any other non-violent infraction.

This is the sequence of a Mini:

- When you notice your child doing something naughty, use the word "Mini" in a short sentence using the One-Word-Per-Year-of-Life guideline. (Examples: "No! Mini" for a 2-year-old or "Not listening, Mini" for a 3-year-old.)

- The child must immediately stop what he is doing and sit on the floor with criss-crossed legs and hands folded in his lap.

- Once his bottom hits the floor, the child must count aloud from 1 to 10 slowly while you stand by quietly.

- After the child finishes counting, he may stand up.

- You repeat your original instruction using a minimum of words.

- The child must perform the original request.

- Once he complies, you both continue on as if nothing happened.

Don't lecture or try to teach your child about what led to the Mini. You've already used up your words, so do not talk about what happened. Remember, we teach when our children are being good, not when they are naughty.

That's it. That's the Mini.

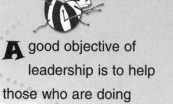

A good objective of leadership is to help those who are doing poorly to do well and to help those who are doing well do even better.

– Jim Rohn,
motivational speaker

The Mini is very effective and convenient because it can be done anytime, anywhere. Your child can perform a Mini in the grocery store, at the mall, in the park, even at the dinner table. The Mini will begin to work when your child realizes that this step is paired with even tougher consequences (Chair and Time-Out) and a more drastic loss of mommy and daddy's attention.

Now, let's look at a Mini in action. Remember Julie, the egg-throwing 5-year-old? This is what would have happened if Mommy had given her a Mini to teach her to stop throwing eggs:

Mommy walks in and catches Julie tossing eggs at the refrigerator. She stops, looks at Julie and, using the One-Word-Per-Year-of-Life rule, says "Julie! Stop throwing eggs. Mini." Julie stops what she is doing and immediately sits down on the kitchen floor, with criss-crossed legs and hands neatly folded in her lap. Mommy stands by without talking. Julie then counts slowly from 1 to 10 and stands up. Next, Mommy says, "Clean up the eggs, Julie." As Julie cleans up the mess, Mommy stands by quietly and helps only when necessary, but she does not talk or lecture about the incident. Once the eggs are cleaned up, Julie and Mommy are both free to go about their day.

The Mini — Rules for Parents:

- If your child is too young to count to 10, counting to 3 or 4 is okay. The purpose of the count is to stop your child in his tracks and get him to focus away from his naughty behavior.

- If your child wears diapers, sitting with criss-crossed legs can be uncomfortable, if not impossible, so sitting with legs straight out is okay.

- You should never allow your child to repeat a Mini; he must do it correctly the first time, EVERY TIME.

- It is very important that your child perform his Minis the same way EVERY TIME. Consistency helps set a pattern and lets your child know what is expected of him.

- You must keep your words to an absolute minimum EVERY TIME.

- Your child must sit down immediately (within 1 to 2 seconds) EVERY TIME.

- She must count slowly and clearly EVERY TIME.

- The closer you follow the rules each and EVERY TIME, the better the Mini will work.

Please note that once the Mini is over, the child must still comply with your original request. The Mini itself isn't enough to change behavior. You still need to follow through and make your child obey. You must also remember that after your child finishes his Mini, it is in the past. Your child did his time, so you should go on as if nothing out of the ordinary has happened. Don't dwell on the negative; spend your time emphasizing the positive.

> To have a good life, it is not enough to remove what is wrong with it. We also need a positive goal, otherwise, why keep going.
>
> – Mihaly Csikszentmihalyi, psychologist

Complete cooperation from your child during a Mini is essential. If she counts too quickly, starts counting before she is sitting, skips numbers, mumbles, refuses to comply with your original request or otherwise messes with the rules, she then moves on to Step 2 – The Chair.

THE CHAIR

The chair is a bit harder than a mini for the child to perform because it shifts much of the control from the child to the parent. If your child refuses to complete his Mini or if he performs his Mini unsuccessfully, the child goes directly to Chair.

This is the sequence of a Chair:

- When it's time to move to the Chair, look at your child and simply say, "Chair."

- The child must immediately walk to a previously designated chair, stool or sofa and sit down with legs still and hands in her lap.

- She must sit still and silent while you stand by quietly. This time, you set the time frame by counting to 10 in your head or by watching a clock. Do not look directly at the child during this time, but be aware of her body movements.

- After you finish counting silently, repeat your original instruction using a minimum of words (say something like, "Now, pick up the book").

- Your child may then get up and perform the task. Once she complies, she is finished. You can both continue on as if nothing happened.

The Mini and the Chair offer short, effective ways to discipline your child. These are excellent methods of self-calming for the child and the parent because they give both of you time to think before taking action. Although the period of time spent in silence is very, very short, it makes a lasting impact on the child. Building on an unsuccessful Mini by following it up with a Chair also shows the child that if he doesn't comply the first time, he will be given another, more serious consequence.

Now, let's look at the Chair in action. Remember Katie, the 2-year-old lipstick lover? This is how Mama could have taught her right from wrong using the Mini/Chair combo:

Mama walks in and sees Katie slathering red lipstick all over her face. She stops, looks at Katie and, using the One-Word-Per-Year-of-Life rule, says, "No! Mini." Katie drops the lipstick and sits down, but she refuses to count and won't keep her hands in her lap. Mama knows Katie is not

> The reason grandchildren and grandparents get along so well is because they share a common enemy.
>
> – Sam Levens, humorist

following the rules, so she looks at her and says, "Chair." Katie then walks to a stool in the kitchen, sits quietly with her hands in her lap and waits without talking or fidgeting. Mama follows Katie into the kitchen, but does not talk or look directly at the child while counting silently from 1 to 10. After Mama finishes counting in her head, she looks at Katie and says, "Clean up." Katie then washes her face with Mama's (silent and limited) assistance and goes on with her day.

The Chair — Rules for Parents:

- Choose a low, kid-friendly chair that the child cannot easily tip over if she kicks and fidgets. A stool, bench or small chair works well.

- Do not use a child's high chair.

- While the child completes her Chair, she is not allowed to mumble, fidget, sing, talk, whine, cry or do anything else that is distracting.

- You should not talk to the child, so stand by silently with no verbal or physical interaction.

- You are the one who does the counting during the Chair, not your child, and be sure to count in your head so you remain completely silent. This little detail puts all of the control in your hands, thus making the Chair a little more severe than a Mini.

- The time period should be short. Use 10 seconds as a guideline, but do not go any longer than 15 seconds. A punishment tends to lose its effectiveness the longer it continues.

- Your child must sit very still during her Chair session. Children who have a hard time sitting still under most circumstances may need just 3 or 4 seconds to feel the effects of this step, so feel free to adjust the time to suit your child.

- Anything other than total compliance with the Chair moves your child up to the next level. If he takes his time walking to the chair, kicks his feet, talks, wiggles or does anything else that breaks the rules, he moves on to Step 3 – The Time-Out.

THE TIME-OUT

The Time-Out is the highest level of our 3-step disciplinary method. It should be used if your child refuses to complete a Chair correctly. You should send your child directly to Time-Out and bypass the Mini and Chair steps if he throws a temper tantrum, commits a very serious offense (like aggression or profanity) or exhibits unsafe behavior (like running into the street or playing with matches).

This is the sequence of a Time-Out:

- When it's time to enforce a Time-Out, look at your child and incorporate the word "Time-Out" into the One-Word-Per-Year-of-Life rule.

- The child must immediately walk to a previously designated quiet area and sit on a specific spot chosen by you with criss-crossed legs, hands in lap.

- He must sit still and silent for 30 seconds while you stand by quietly. You set the time frame by counting in your head or by watching a clock. Do not look directly at the child during this time, but be aware of his body movements. Do not talk no matter what the child does or says.

- The Time-Out does not begin until the child is sitting correctly and silently on his spot. Restart the clock if he cries, throws a tantrum, pouts, whines, giggles or does anything other than sit quietly on his spot.

- After 30 seconds of complete silence have passed, repeat your original instruction using a minimum of words.

- Your child may then leave the room and perform the task. Once he complies, he is finished. You can both continue on as if nothing happened. If he does not comply, begin another Time-Out.

As you can see, the Time-Out is more severe than the Mini and the Chair because it results in a more dramatic loss of parental attention. Increasing the period of silence and moving the child to a "quiet room" will help him understand that you are in control of the situation. The Time-Out also helps teach your child valuable lessons about self-calming that will serve him far into the future.

Now, let's look at the Time-Out in action. Remember Ian, the messy little 6-year-old who refused to clean his room? Had his father chosen to give the boy a Mini/Chair/Time-Out consequence, the interaction could have unfolded something like this:

Dad asks Ian to pick up his room and the boy says, "No." Dad sees this as blatant disobedience, so he says, "Not listening. Mini." (Notice how Dad uses the fewest words possible.) Ian says, "No," and refuses to sit down.

Dad then says, "Chair." (Dad once again uses very few words.) Ian walks to the chair, but instead of sitting on it, he climbs up and stands on top of it.

Dad then decides a Time-Out is justified, so he says, "Ian, Time-Out," while gently leading the boy to his room. (Gently is the key word in this sentence. Lightly touching Ian on the back as he follows the boy down the hallway is appropriate. Grabbing the child in anger and directing him hastily toward the room is not acceptable.) Ian then walks to a pillow in a corner, sits on it with criss-crossed legs and hands in lap. He sits quietly with a minimum of movement while Dad stands silently outside the bedroom door. Dad does not look directly at Ian, but he remains aware of the boy's movements while looking at his watch. (See how Dad maintains closeness to the boy and monitors his actions without paying direct attention to him?)

If your parents never had children, chances are you won't either.

– Dick Cavett,
Humorist

After 30 seconds have passed, Dad looks at Ian and says, "Okay. Now clean your room." (Dad follows through with the teaching plan by asking Ian to complete his original request.) Ian then gets up and picks up his toys. The Time-Out session is over after Ian finishes cleaning his room. (Remember, Ian must pick up his toys before this incident is considered complete.)

This example illustrates what to expect after you and your child have been using the Time-Out process for a while. Please don't expect your child to complete the 3-step process this way from the beginning. It takes time and practice to get to this point. Your child will learn through repetition what he needs to do to get out of the Time-Out area, so you must stick to your guns. You must teach to the situation every time, and, in the process, your child gains control of himself by learning valuable listening and coping strategies.

Time-Out Problems

The sequence of the Time-Out may sound simple, but many parents find several aspects of the sequence hard to enforce. You may find it difficult to keep quiet when your child is acting up during a Time-Out, but it is very important that you refrain from talking. Remember, part of the punishment is taking away your attention, so if you talk and explain your way through this step, you defeat the purpose.

You may also find that the first few times your child is placed in Time-Out, he will probably throw a tantrum and refuse to immediately sit on the spot. Face it, the kid is mad. When he was naughty in the past, you inadvertently gave him attention by yelling, explaining and negotiating, but now he is getting no attention because you are not talking. He may run around the room, grab toys, try to get out of the room, spit, throw a tantrum or do anything else to avoid succumbing to your rules.

When this happens (and believe us, it will!), you should very gently and quietly redirect him back to the spot without talking. The child knows what you want him to do, so use no words.

> The good you do today may be quickly forgotten, but the impact of what you do will never disappear.
>
> – Unknown

Because the Time-Out does not start until the child is sitting properly and quietly on his spot, you may find yourself getting angry and anxious too, but don't give in. No matter how angry you or your child gets, DO NOT let him out of the room until he successfully completes his 30-second Time-Out. You must stand your ground, so focus your energy on keeping yourself quiet. Now, we aren't going to lie. This can be very challenging. Your child's first Time-Outs will be tough on both of you, and the experience will get worse before it gets better. Some parents who've utilized this step successfully find the first few days very trying but worth the effort. If you hang in there and provide little attention, these episodes will decrease over time.

> **O**ur earth is degenerate in these latter days; bribery and corruption are common; children no longer obey their parents; and the end of the world is evidently approaching.
> – Assyrian clay tablets 2800 BC

Once a child learns and understands the Time-Out process, he realizes that the sooner he conforms, the better. It's like a light bulb switching on when a child figures this out. When told to complete a Time-Out, these "enlightened" children drop what they are doing, walk quickly to the Time-Out space, sit down and wait quietly for the parent's permission to get up. Once given the go-ahead, they jump up, complete the original request and get on with their day. At this point, some parents begin to feel the punishment isn't harsh enough because the child isn't "suffering" for his actions. Please don't fall into this trap. When your child gets to this point, you should celebrate! This is your goal! You have successfully taught him how to listen to you and calm himself. "Suffering" shouldn't enter into the equation. We teach with love, remember? Not with pain.

Although these steps may sound simple to master, please remember: If at any time you feel this process is too much for you, or if you feel your child is unsafe, stop the Time-Out session immediately and seek professional help.

Time-Out Safety

It is absolutely essential that you realize the importance of safety during the Time-Out process. The most important concern is that the child is in a safe place with proper ventilation where he cannot get hurt. Good options include a hallway, corner or any uninteresting area. If a bedroom or other multi-purpose room is used, designate a specific spot to serve as the Time-Out area. You can mark the spot with a pillow or carpet square, tape off an "X" on the floor or use any other marker that makes it clear to the child that this is where he is expected to sit in the event of a Time-Out. If you choose a corner, it is not necessary for the child to face the corner.

You should also consider your child's individual coping mechanisms before choosing a Time-Out area. If your son is a "runner" who tends to flee when he is angry, don't choose a spot near steps or a door; if your daughter is a "banger" who hits her head or hands when she is mad, be sure to steer clear of glass windows, doors and tables; if your son is a "pouter" who

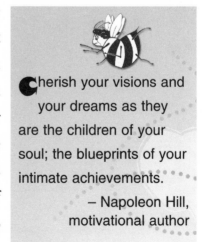

Cherish your visions and your dreams as they are the children of your soul; the blueprints of your intimate achievements.

– Napoleon Hill, motivational author

tends to withdraw when he is angry, just about any place is acceptable as long as he is safe.

Choosing your Time-Out spot wisely also helps avoid unnecessary accidents. By the time your child reaches the point where he needs a Time-Out, he will be angry and may look for a way to get your attention. He may even try something drastic, like climbing a dresser or playing with electrical outlets, to get you to intervene. That's why you should create a Time-Out space that is as barren as possible, and you should check the area regularly for items that may endanger an angry child.

Window coverings, cords, pencils, glasses, mirrors or any other potentially dangerous items should be removed from the area before your child's first Time-Out. You should also make sure that the child does not have access to windows that can be opened or broken. And remember, you should never leave your child unattended during a Time-Out under any circumstances.

If your child hurts himself during a Time-Out, assess whether the child is actually hurt and if the injury needs immediate attention. If your child is faking an injury or if the injury is very minor (like a small scratch or stubbed toe), continue with the Time-Out. If the child's injury needs your attention, end the session immediately, attend to the wound and assess whether you should continue with the Time-Out session.

Some children will do anything, including intentionally hurting themselves, to get out of a Time-Out. If you even suspect that your child has hurt himself on purpose as a way to take control of the Time-Out session, you should contact a mental health professional for guidance. A situation like this one is a strong indicator that you and your child need extra help and shouldn't continue on a teaching system without professional assistance.

Here are a few more unbendable rules to consider when choosing a Time-Out space:

- No television

- No books

- No video games

- No food

- No phone

- No lock on the door

- No interaction with siblings or friends

NEVER, EVER LEAVE YOUR CHILD UNATTENDED!

Time-Out – Rules for Parents

Time-Outs tend to work better if the parent stays in or just outside the room during the session. It is important to avoid eye contact, but it is just as important to keep tabs on your child and his body movements. You can accomplish this by focusing on his body, not on his eyes.

Do not talk, coach, prompt or remind your child how to perform the Time-Out correctly.

If the child does not immediately cooperate and refuses to sit on his spot, wait quietly until he complies. He will figure out that he is stuck in the room until he cooperates, so be patient.

Some parents enforce a One-Minute-Per-Year-of-Life guideline when using Time-Outs. There is no research that supports this principle. Expecting a 7-year-old to sit quietly and still for 7 minutes sets you up for failure. Even 2 minutes is an eternity for a child. Using a shorter, 30-second time period is doable for the youngster, and it provides greater, more consistent results.

The Time-Out process can be frustrating for the parent, so come up with some coping mechanisms of your own. Read a book, leaf through a magazine, listen to music using headphones, do sit-ups, play solitaire, make lists, anything that will help you keep your cool, while allowing you to keep an eye on your youngster. Some parents keep a Time-Out journal nearby to help them express their feelings, log their child's reactions and document how long each Time-Out lasts.

The Magic of the Mini

Once your child learns the entire 3-step Mini/Chair/Time-Out process, she will realize that if she performs her Mini correctly the first time, her disciplinary period is over. This is a win/win situation for everyone. The parent learns to control the child's naughty behavior by saying one simple word; the child learns that she can avoid the toughest step of the process (Time-Out) by responding to the Mini. The Chair simply offers one more opportunity for the child to comply. All of this results in a calm, loving method of teaching right from wrong with no yelling, screaming or crying. See? Everybody wins.

Good friends are good for your health.
– Irwin Sarason, professor of psychology

Is This Process Mean or Harmful?

Some parents wonder if this process is mean, unloving or even harmful to their children. If you are one of these people, then try looking at it this way: The worst thing you are doing is asking your child to stop her naughty behavior, sit down and count to 10. That's all. You are not yelling, spanking, belittling or worse. Making a conscious effort to refrain from talking during the extremely short time it takes to complete a Mini, Chair or Time-Out is much better than over-reacting, and it shows your child that problems can be worked out in a calm, civilized manner.

There is nothing either good or bad but thinking makes it so.

– William Shakespeare

This process is a valuable parental tool, and when you learn to use it correctly, you'll realize just how loving and effective this method can be. It teaches your child that he gets what he wants when he is good and gets little to nothing when he is naughty. After all, isn't that how life should be?

FAST FACTS

- All kids have their naughty moments. The key to managing these unfavorable behaviors lies in how you choose to respond to them.

- It is normal for parents to do whatever it takes to stop naughty behavior as quickly as possible, but avoiding a bad reaction from your child is not an effective way to teach your child right from wrong.

- You must gain control by determining how you plan to deal with the everyday ups and downs of parenting. Remember, you are the primary teacher in your child's life; it is your duty to teach him right from wrong. If you tackle these issues now, you'll both enjoy the benefits for years to come.

- It is important to deal with naughty behaviors immediately so the child has the opportunity to learn from his mistakes.

- Never warn your child of an impending consequence. The words you use when threatening your child go "in one ear and out the other." These warnings also give her more of what she really wants – your attention.

Choosing when to talk and when to stay silent is one of the most important decisions a parent can make. Pouring on the attention when your child is good and limiting your words when he is naughty will set up a strong contrast between what he experiences when he is good and how things change when he is disobedient.

The One-Word-Per-Year-of-Life guideline is easy to remember, simple to enforce and allows you to teach your child while offering a minimum of attention and language.

Giving consequences to young children can be tricky because there is no possession a parent can take away that a young child can't easily replace. Your undivided attention is priceless because your child cannot replace it. That's why limiting your words and actions during the naughty times is so effective.

Scolding and yelling are not effective consequences. You'll see much more progress using a calm, controlled response.

The 3-step method taught in this book discourages naughty behavior, controls anger and strengthens the relationship between you and your child.

The first step, called the Mini, is used when a child first shows a naughty behavior, like not listening, refusing to obey, ignoring a request or any other non-violent infraction.

The second step, called the Chair, is used if your child refuses to complete a Mini or if he performs his Mini unsuccessfully.

The third step, called the Time-Out, is used if your child refuses to complete a Chair correctly, throws a temper tantrum, commits a very serious offense (like aggression or profanity) or exhibits unsafe behavior (like running into the street or playing with matches).

These steps, along with the careful use of your attention, work together to create a blueprint for handling inappropriate behavior.

If at any time during this process you feel this is too much for you, or if you feel your child is unsafe, stop the Time-Out process and seek professional help.

Get Ready...Get Set

Now that you've read about the basics of our program, it's time to put these principles into action, but wait! Before you get started, grab a piece of paper and a pencil, sit down in a cozy chair and spend the next few minutes completing the Are You Ready?

Are you Ready? Quiz:

1. How many times should you read this book cover to cover before establishing this program into your household?

2. What is the one thing your child wants most?

3. Why is practice important when learning a new skill or behavior?

4. When is the best time to teach your child proper behavior using your words and attention? Why?

5. What is the difference between Time-In and Time-Out?

6. Is it Okay to wait a minute or two to praise your child for good behavior? Why or why not?

7. What is the difference between neutral and developing behaviors?

8. Name 5 ways to praise and reward your child verbally, physically and materially.

9. What is your favorite color? (Okay, that's a trick question. We just wanted to make sure you were still paying attention.)

10. Name 3 mistakes parents make when dealing with inappropriate behavior in their children?

11. What is the One-Word-Per-Year-of-Life guideline? Why is it important?

12. Is yelling and screaming at your child an acceptable consequence? Why or why not?

13. What is a Mini?

14. What is a Chair?

15. What is a Time-Out?

16. What is the "Magic of the Mini?"

17. What should you do if you feel this process is too much for you or if your child is in danger?

Now check your answers in the Resources section in the back of this book.

How did you do? If you answered every question correctly, congratulations! You are officially ready to begin using this process with your children. If you answered even one question incorrectly,

Neither fire nor wind, birth nor death can erase our good deeds.

– Buddha

PLEASE go back and clarify that topic before proceeding. You will find the corresponding page numbers listed alongside the correct answer in the Resources section.

It is essential that you understand each and every aspect of this program before using it on your children because all of the components work together to give you the long-lasting results you are looking for. So if you have any questions about the process, go back right now and reread the sections you need to brush up on. You'll be glad you did.

Exercises: The Journey

Due to the love and affection, discipline and structure, my son is now ready to face the world and has a wonderful foundation in which to grow. It has also given me the tools to keep this up.

— A grateful parent

As you move toward improving your child's behavior, you must also work on improving your own behavior, as well. This exercise will focus on preparing you to carry out Minis, Chairs and Time-Outs in a calm, parental fashion. The way we will do this is to have you practice how you will react in teaching situations.

First, find a private place with a mirror where you will not be disturbed. Designate this as your parent's practice time. Now, prepare yourself to give your child a Mini by deciding exactly what you will say when a naughty situation comes up. For example, if your child is 6 years old, decide exactly what 6 words you will use the next time he interrupts you while you are on the phone. You might choose, "Jimmy, Mini. No interrupting phone calls," or something of that nature. After you have chosen your 6 words, look into the mirror and say them to your reflection. Be firm, but not angry. Keep your face calm by relaxing your eyebrows and softening your jaw. Maintain your composure by breathing deeply. After you feel good about your performance, move on to choosing words for a Chair and a Time-Out. Repeat your phrases as many times as necessary until you feel comfortable and secure. Repeat this parent's practice session until you are confident that you are limiting your words and following the other rules set out in this chapter.

You can also help yourself by setting up 5 ways to cope during difficult Time-Outs. Grab your notebook and brainstorm some ideas that would keep you calm during this often trying time. Write your ideas down so you can refer to them when you need them. Another great idea is to find a spot near your child's Time-Out space and stock it with things that could serve as distractions if you need them. Your Time-Out stockpile might consist of a couple of new magazines, a journal and pen, your best friend's phone number and an exercise mat for sit-ups. You can also put your items in a basket or box so you can move them from place to place more easily. These little "life lines" can be invaluable when your child is uncooperative or if a Time-Out gets lengthy.

7

Successful Teaching that Lasts a Lifetime

Congratulations! You are about to embark on a journey that will change your relationship with your child forever. You are now armed with the skills it takes to implement a proven teaching method into your home that will decrease naughty actions, increase acceptable behavior and cement the bond between you and your child. You should feel proud of the fact that you care enough about your child to learn and implement these skills. Give yourself a pat on the back. You deserve it!

> Children have never been very good at listening to adults, but they have never failed to imitate them.
> – James Baldwin, American Novelist

Explaining the Process

Now that you know what you are doing, it's time to teach these techniques to your child. The best way to start the process is to spend the first 3 days praising your child whenever you see him doing something good. Use the guidelines outlined in chapter 4, and be sure to refer to the suggestions in the Resources Section for some creative ways to give praise.

> I am not caused by my history — my parents, my childhood and development. These are the mirrors in which I may catch glimpses of my image.
>
> – James Hillman
> psychologist

On the fourth day, sit down with your child and explain that, from now on, your household is working under a new set of rules. Explain the different steps to her (Mini, Chair and Time-Out) and exactly what you expect from her in each situation. Take the time to practice each step so she knows what to do, then explain what will happen if she wiggles, cries, does not listen or otherwise disobeys the rules. You should practice Minis, Chairs and Time-Outs several times a day during calm, cooperative moments for the first few weeks until she understands the rules and knows what is happening.

You'll be much more successful if you make these practice sessions fun and engaging. Incorporate laughter and excitement, but be sure to let her know that the process must not be taken lightly. Give her tons of praise for completing each practice session so she knows she is doing it correctly, and make sure you follow the exact same pattern each and every time, so there is no confusion on her part or yours. Your youngster will enjoy these practice sessions and look forward to them because she gets valuable attention from you.

It is important that you continue practicing and reviewing these concepts, even after you are using the steps, until you are satisfied that your child understands what is expected of her. Keep in mind that if she has practiced successfully, then suddenly forgets what to do when you call for a Mini or Chair, she is being disobedient and you must act accordingly.

Giant Leaps Forward, Baby Steps Back

Once your child learns the ins and outs of the Mini, Chair and Time-Out processes, you are home free, right? Well, unfortunately, it's not that simple. Your child will occasionally regress and will either revisit her old behaviors or add new ones just to make sure the rules haven't changed. It's in her nature to

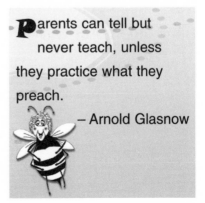

Parents can tell but never teach, unless they practice what they preach.

– Arnold Glasnow

continue testing you, so be ready for it. When you notice she is acting out in new ways, trust your gut. Ask yourself what your initial reaction is regarding the behavior and act accordingly. If you sense that the action breaks your rules, even a little bit, then give a consequence. Remember: It doesn't hurt to give a consequence when you're unsure, but if you fail to act when you should, you are asking for trouble. So if you stick to your guns and listen to your gut, you'll both reap the benefits.

It's also important for you to know that regressing into old behaviors isn't always the child's fault. Often times, the parent is the one who regresses, thereby causing the child to fall back into his old, naughty behaviors. If you relax the rules, change the procedure, ease up on praising and rewarding, lengthen or shorten the Time-Out period, let one or two misbehaviors "slide" or otherwise modify the steps to suit your needs, your child will think he can go back to his old ways too. This can set you and your child back significantly, so try your best to stay on track. Don't give up! It will get worse before it gets better, but trust us, your child is worth the sacrifice.

A Beautiful Beginning

Now, take a deep breath in, exhale slowly and let a big smile cover your face. You did it! You are ready! You possess the knowledge and skills you need to start a bright new future with your child today. Sure, he'll get into trouble, and he'll undoubtedly continue to "push your buttons" on a regular basis, but now you know how to turn these naughty actions into powerful teaching moments in a way that will strengthen and enhance your family relationship forever.

Exercises:
Where do you
want to go next?

I now know how to break the cycle of rage without getting angry and sucked into my daughter's rage. My wife and I also have valuable parenting tools and techniques that help us maximize our parenting skills. We have reached our goals and obtained the results that we desired with our little girl.

– A grateful parent

Once you have worked your way through improving your child's most troubling behavior, you should feel extremely proud of yourself and your child. It is difficult to make changes like those you have already made, so don't let this moment go by unnoticed. Celebrate your accomplishments together by taking your child out for an ice cream cone, enjoying a movie or taking a walk. Take a moment to tell your child how proud you are of him and how much fun it is to work together to solve problems. By sharing and connecting with your child, you will grow closer together and you will find conquering your next hurdle much easier.

Speaking of your next hurdle, how about pulling out that list of target behaviors and choosing your next goal? Once you decide which goal you want to tackle next, follow the same process outlined in these exercises until the next developing behavior becomes a solid, neutral behavior. You'll find that once you have succeeded with your first, most difficult behavior, the others will seem more attainable.

It is easy to let ourselves slide into old habits, especially if things are going well, but you need to keep the concepts outlined in this book on the "front burner" to avoid slip-ups and back-slides. So take a moment right now and pull out a calendar. Look forward to the date that is exactly 2 months from today and make a big star on that date. This is the day we want you to pick this book up and reread it from cover to cover again as a refresher course. Revisiting these concepts often will help you stay on track and keep motivated. If you need

In raising my children, I have lost my mind but found my soul.

– Lisa T. Shepherd

to refer to the book before the 2 months are up, then by all means, do so! But be sure to keep this book close at hand and pick it up every few months.

As you sit here reading these words, your child is somewhere waiting for your love and guidance. Right now, he is hoping you will walk up, give him a hug and tell him how much you love and appreciate him. So put this book down and go hug your child. Look into his sweet eyes and tell him how much you love him. The miracle of parenthood is yours for the taking. The tools you learned from this book will help you find the loving relationship you and your child deserve.

Resources:
50 Low-Cost and No-Cost
Rewards for Children

A treat from the "ice cream man" truck

Trip to the park

Help wash the car

Extra bedtime story

Feed the pet

Ring a bell

Piggyback ride

Finger play game

Take video or a photo of child to show how good he is

Eat outside

Choose a game to play with mom or dad

Help parent complete a task

Bubble bath

Whirling in a circle in parent's arms

Finger paint

Blow bubbles

Resources

Bounce on the bed

Stay up late

Trip to the zoo

Twirling in an office chair

Look at the stars

Help hold the baby/puppy/kitty

Go swimming

Get pulled in a wagon

Carry purse or suitcase

Stroke hair

Give a wink

Praise your child to someone else in her presence

Stars on a chart

Money for piggy bank

Play dress-up in mom or dad's clothing

Spend the night with grandparent or friend

Go to a sporting event

Eat dinner in a restaurant

Run errand alone with dad or mom

Resources

Bake cookies or brownies

Plan a day's activities

Choose a special TV program

Skip a chore for a day

Call someone on the telephone

Setting the table

Camp in the backyard or in his own bedroom

String beads

Movie night at home

Play favorite music

Color in a special coloring book

Choose the menu for a meal

Handshakes

Decorate cake or cupcakes

Get a special sticker

Resources:
List of Social Skills or Acceptable Ways to Handle Certain Situations

Following instructions/listening

1. Say "Okay."

2. Do what Daddy asks right away.

Accepting a "No" answer

1. Say "Okay, Mommy."

Asking for Help

1. Don't get angry or mad.

2. Say "Please help me, Dad."

3. Say "Thank you."

Asking Permission

1. Stay calm.

2. Say "Please may I _____?"

Apologizing

1. Say "I'm sorry I _____ "

Interrupting

1. Tap dad gently on the arm one time or say "Excuse me" calmly one time.

2. Wait quietly for an answer.

Sharing

1. Ask other child "May I please play with you?"

2. Wait for answer.

3. If the answer is yes, take turns with the toys.

4. If the answer is no, walk away or ask mom for help.

"Are You Ready?"
Quiz Answers

1. It is essential that you read this entire book at least once, cover to cover, before beginning the process.

2. The one thing your child desires most is you (page 9).

3. Repeated performance results in a more successful outcome. You become more proficient at the actions you perform most frequently (page20).

4. The most effective time to teach proper behavior is when your child is being good because this is when he is most open to you and your suggestions (page13).

5. Time-In describes the process of giving a child positive attention or small material rewards (like a cookie or penny) immediately following developing and neutral behaviors (page 36).

    Time-Out is a widely utilized disciplinary method that moves a child into a quiet area for calming in the event of naughty behavior (page 35).

6. It is imperative that you give praise directly following your child's positive or neutral behavior.

Why? Because humans learn by consequence, so we see our circumstances as directly related to our actions. This is how we learn (page 42).

7. Neutral behaviors are actions your child already does well. These are skills the youngster has already mastered and performs as a matter of habit (page 23).

   Developing behaviors are any new skills you are working to teach your child. These desired actions include any first-time activity or response that is positive, helpful or simply acceptable (page 40).

8. Verbal praises include phrases like, "Good job," "Atta boy," "I'm so proud of you," "You are getting so big," and "Thank you." Physical praises include hugs, kisses, high-fives, doing a "happy dance," jumping up and down, or helping you complete a task. Material rewards include a penny, sucker, animal cracker or other small symbol. See the Resources Section for more ideas (page 133).

9. We just wanted to lighten things up a bit with this trick question. According to www.color-wheel-pro.com, if your favorite color is black, you're mysterious. Purple? You're extravagant. Blue? You're trustworthy. Yellow? You're cheerful. Orange? You're creative. Red? You're emotionally intense.

10. Talking too much (pages 85, 104); clowning around (page 71); negotiating (page 104); repeating requests (page 71); not giving a consequence (page 128); scolding and yelling (page 81); giving in to temper tantrums (page 86); warning the child (page 84).

11. The total number of words you use should equal your child's age. This rule is easy to remember, simple to enforce and allows you to teach your child while offering a minimum of attention and language (page 78).

12. No. The effects of verbal confrontations do not last, they rarely result in a decrease in naughty behavior and they tend to work against a parent's authority. A calm, controlled response is much more effective (page 82).

13. The very first step in the disciplinary sequence is called the Mini. A Mini is used when a child first shows a naughty behavior, like not listening, refusing to obey, ignoring a request or any other non-violent infraction (page 90). See page 92 for an example of a Mini.

14. The Chair is the second step in our disciplinary sequence. It is used when your child refuses to complete a Mini or if he performs his Mini unsuccessfully (page 95). See page 97 for an example of a Chair.

15. The Time-Out is the highest level of our 3-step disciplinary method. It should be used if your child refuses to complete a Chair correctly, throws a temper tantrum, commits a very serious offense (like aggression or profanity) or exhibits unsafe behavior (like running into the street or playing with matches) (page 100). See page 102 for an example of a Time-Out.

16. Once your child learns the entire 3-step Mini/Chair/Time-Out process, she will realize that if she performs her Mini correctly the first time, her disciplinary period is over. This is a win/win situation for everyone (page 111).

17. If you ever feel this process is too much for you, or if you feel your child is unsafe, stop the Time-Out process and seek professional help (page 106).